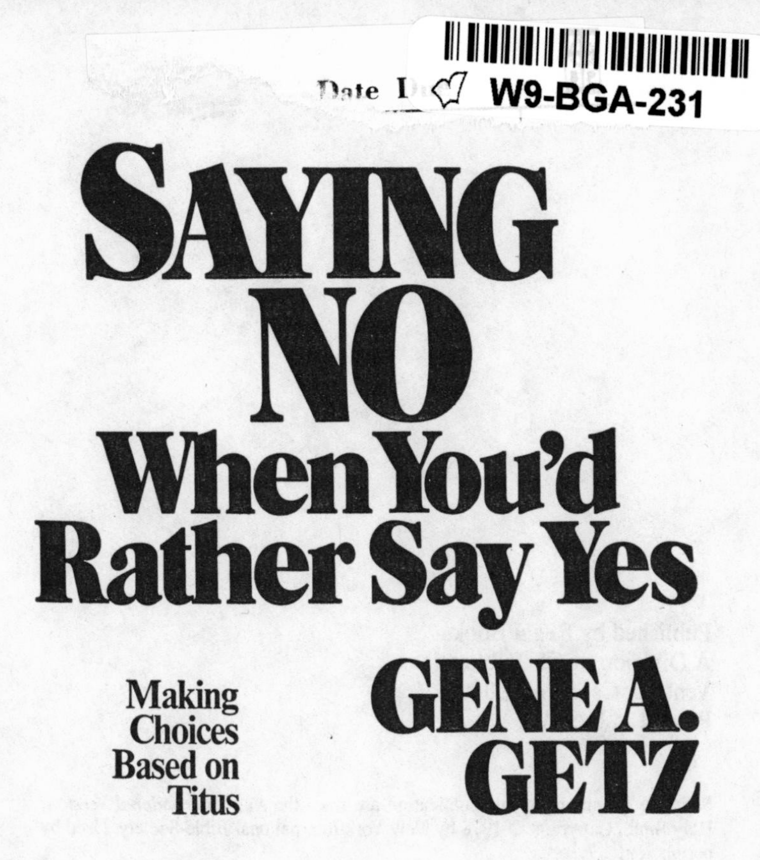

SAYING NO When You'd Rather Say Yes

Making Choices Based on Titus

GENE A. GETZ

Regal Books
A Division of GL Publications
Ventura, California, U.S.A.

Published by Regal Books
A Division of GL Publications
Ventura, California 93006
Printed in U.S.A.

Second Edition

Library of Congress Cataloging in Publication Data applied for.

2 3 4 5 6 7 8 9 10 / 91 90 89 88 87

Rights for publishing this book in other languages are contracted by Gospel Literature International (GLINT) foundation. GLINT also provides technical help for the adaptation, translation, and publishing of Bible study resources and books in scores of languages worldwide. For further information, contact GLINT, Post Office Box 488, Rosemead, California, 91770, U.S.A., or the publisher.

Contents

RENEWAL–A BIBLICAL PERSPECTIVE

This study in Paul's letter to Titus is another book in the Biblical Renewal Series. Renewal is the essence of dynamic Christianity and the basis on which Christians, both in a corporate or Body sense and as individual believers, can determine the will of God. Paul made this clear when he wrote to the Roman Christians—"be transformed by the renewing of your mind. Then," he continued, "you will be able to test and approve what God's will is" (Rom. 12:2). Here Paul is talking about renewal in both a personal and a corporate sense. In other words, Paul is asking these Christians as a Body of believers to develop the mind of Christ through corporate renewal.

Personal renewal will not happen as God intended it unless it happens in the context of corporate renewal. On the other hand, corporate renewal will not happen as God intended without personal renewal. Both are necessary.

The larger circle represents Church Renewal. This is the most comprehensive concept in the New Testament. However, every local *church* is made up of smaller self-contained, but interrelated units. The *family* in Scripture emerges as the church in miniature. In turn, the family is made up of an even smaller social unit—*marriage*. The third inner circle represents *personal* renewal, which is inseparably linked to all of the other basic units. Marriage is made up of two separate individuals who become one. The family is made up of parents and children who are also to reflect the mind of Christ. And the church is made up of not only individual Christians, but couples and families.

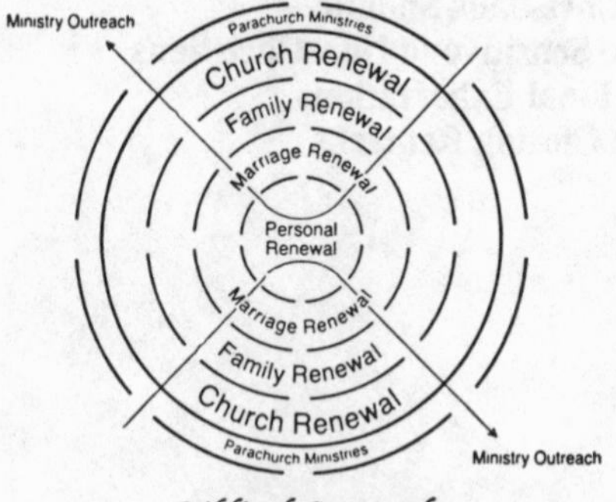

Biblical Renewal

Though all of these social units are interrelated, biblical renewal can begin within any specific social unit. But wherever it begins—in the church, families, marriages or individuals—the process immediately touches all the other social units. And one thing is certain: All that God says is consistent and harmonious. He does not have one set of principles for the church and another set for the family, another for husbands and wives, and another for individual Christians. For example, the principles God outlines for local church elders, fathers and husbands, regarding their role as leaders, are interrelated and consistent. If they are not, we can be sure that we have not interpreted God's plan accurately.

This book is a study both in corporate and personal renewal. It begins with you as an individual Christian and demonstrates how you can grow spiritually in the context of a dynamic body of believers.

The Biblical Renewal Series is an expanding library of books by Gene Getz designed to provide supportive help in moving toward renewal. Each of these books fits into one of the circles described above and will provoke thought, provide interaction and tangible steps toward growth.

ONE ANOTHER SERIES

Building Up One Another

Encouraging One Another

Loving One Another

PERSONALITY SERIES

Abraham
David
Joseph
Joshua
Moses
Nehemiah

THE MEASURE OF SERIES

Church
Family
Man
Marriage
Woman

BIBLE BOOK SERIES
Ephesians, Philippians, 1 Thessalonians, Titus, James

Sharpening the Focus of the Church presents an overall perspective for Church Renewal. All of these books are available from your bookstore.

Preface

The world is changing! And so are people. Not too many years ago the social values in American culture were almost synonymous with biblical values.

Don't misunderstand! I'm not suggesting we have been a *Christian* nation in the sense of truly following Jesus Christ. However, we *have* been a nation that has historically built its values on the basic and moral teachings that have grown out of the Old and New Testaments. Over the years our basic life styles have reflected these values—in our family life, in our business life, in government, and in the whole area of recreation and entertainment.

In recent years, however, our American value system has changed dramatically. The criteria for determining what is right and wrong no longer focus on the Hebrew-Christian ethic. Many moral and ethical judgments are often made in the light of a relative and changing standard. Marital unfaithfulness and divorce have become an accepted way of life. Cheating in the business world is often considered normal. Moral laxity and dishonesty in government are flagrant and persistent patterns. And movies, television, stage shows, magazines, and books all reflect our changing values.

What about the Christian? What about *your* life style? In the midst of a changing world true believers must be sure they do not become a *part* of the world's system as they live in the *midst* of this system (Rom. 12:1-2).

Paul's letter to Titus provides a study in the life style of a Christian living in a pagan society. What Paul had to say to Titus and the Cretan Christians includes all ages and relates to almost all situations and relationships in life—in the home, in the church, on the job, and in our relationships to government and to non-Christians generally.

This study *can* change your life—not because of this book, but because of *the* Book! Hopefully, all that is written in the pages to follow reflects God's Word and correctly interprets His will for our lives.

GENE A. GETZ
Dallas, Texas

Acknowledgment

A special word of appreciation goes to Mike Cocoris, an Instructor in the Pastoral Ministries Department at Dallas Theological Seminary and Vice President of EvanTell, a unique Bible teaching—evangelistic ministry. Mike first read this manuscript in its unpublished form and not only made helpful suggestions, but also encouraged me greatly by his enthusiastic response to its format and content. Mike is well qualified to review this material since one of his special series of messages that he gives in his evangelistic ministry includes an exposition of Paul's letter to Titus. Thanks, Mike, for your encouragement.

How to Make This Book Work for You

You can use this book in various ways.

Personal Study

First, you can read it by yourself—a chapter at a time. Or you can read it straight through in one sitting if you like. But if you only read it, you will miss the most important thing—the life response and follow-through.

Every chapter leads to a decision on your part—a twentieth-century application to your own life. But *you* must do the applying to your particular situation.

So you will want to study with book, Bible, notebook, and pencil in hand. And you will want to be prepared to think and meditate. That's why if you read it through in one or two sittings, you will need to consider the first reading an overview. Then go back and read carefully one chapter at a time and work through each life response, probably not more than one a week. If you go farther, you'll have more to do than you can handle.

Group Study

Personal study is excellent, and it may be your preference. But the real excitement will come in a group, when you meet as members of the Body of Christ—in a Sunday School class, in midweek Bible study, at a morning coffee hour—and read and discuss the material together. Work out the life responses. Share your personal goals and objectives and work through the group projects.

Family Bible Study

Once a week, with your children who are junior-high age (12 or above), study this book together. Set aside one evening and make it "family night."

A suggestion: Every member of the family should do his "homework" by reading each chapter and working out the life responses in private devotions. Then come together once a week to share your responses and follow through on each suggested "family project."

Enjoy this book! Bible study *can* be exciting—especially when it changes your life.

WHY THIS STUDY OF *TITUS*?

The churches in Crete desperately needed to "develop the mind of Christ." The process of renewal was just starting. Problems permeated the Christian community. False teachers were leading whole households astray.

Paul left Titus in Crete to help these churches mature and grow. The instructions in this little book present a step-by-step process for renewing a church. If these steps worked in Crete, they'll work anywhere on the planet earth.

What about your church? To what extent does it need to "develop the mind of Christ?" Paul's words to Titus are guaranteed to help.

An Overview

For a quick survey of Paul's letter to Titus, you may find it helpful to read the layout at the beginning of each chapter in this book before reading the study material. On the left-hand page you will find the text of the Epistle presented in grammatical form—actually a logical layout. On the opposite page the basic outline included in the text is repeated and expanded into subpoints that also grow out of the message of the Epistle. Thus, as you read through Paul's letter, you will be able to observe how his thoughts and ideas are outlined and developed in this book.

The Format

Each chapter in this book is organized into several parts.

1. Something to Think About

How does your life—as you live in the twentieth century—relate to what Paul was saying to Titus and the Christians living in Crete? To help bridge your thinking from the twentieth to the first century, each chapter begins with "Something to Think About"—some questions, a statement, a quiz, a checklist. Though it will take only a minute to work through these little projects, they will help prepare your heart and mind for the particular passage of Paul's letter you are about to study. These exercises are particularly important in helping you to see how relevant God's Word is to your life right now, wherever you are now and whatever you do!

2. A Look at Paul's Letter

In this section in each chapter the particular segment of the text under study is presented in a grammatical layout. This is designed to help you focus in on a specific segment of the text. (An overview of the entire letter is presented before the opening chapter.)

3. What Did Paul Say?

The detailed outline for the passage under study appears on the opposite page from the grammatical layout of the Bible passage. Thus you can read the Scripture first and then get a quick overview of each idea developed in the remainder of the chapter.

4. What Did Paul Mean?

This exposition of the Bible text is the main part of each chapter. The Scripture passage is explained phrase by phrase, verse by verse, and paragraph by paragraph.

5. A Twentieth-Century Application

Though each chapter begins with *you*—as you live in the twentieth century—here you will move from the first century to the twentieth in more depth. After looking at the actual meaning of Paul's words to Titus and the Cretan Christians, you will observe how his statements apply in a contemporary situation. In other words, what does it mean to us today? Usually this application is general and relevant to all Christians.

6. A Personal Life Response

We dare not stop with a *general* application, even though it is relevant. What goal or goals can you set for *your* life now to apply this biblical truth? With pencil in hand, you will be encouraged to write out an action step.

7. An individual or group project

This final action is a "follow-through" activity—something to do that will take you even farther in understanding what Paul is saying to Titus and the Christians in Crete—*and* to you as a twentieth-century Christian.

Chapter I

Paul's Authority and Responsibility

SOMETHING TO THINK ABOUT

	YES	NO	UNCERTAIN
Twentieth-century Christians should attempt to live in *every respect* like first-century Christians.	☐	☐	☐
Twentieth-century Christians have the same authority as *all* first-century Christians.	☐	☐	☐
Twentieth-century Christians can be involved in an *apostolic* ministry.	☐	☐	☐

A LOOK AT PAUL'S LETTER

Paul's Credentials

1:1 Paul,
a servant of God ———1
and
an apostle of Jesus Christ———2

Paul's Calling

for the faith of God's elect ——1
and
the knowledge of the truth ——2
that leads to godliness—

1:2 a faith
and
knowledge
resting on the hope of eternal life,
which God,
who does not lie,
promised before the beginning of time,

1:3 and
at his appointed season
he brought his word to light
through the preaching
entrusted to me
by the command of God our Savior.

WHAT DID PAUL SAY?

A. Paul's Credentials

1. A servant

2. An apostle

B. Paul's Calling

1. Relative to salvation

2. Relative to sanctification

WHAT DID PAUL MEAN?

Paul began most of his letters with an introduction and greeting that had certain common elements. Usually he identified himself as "an apostle," and also extended "grace and peace" to those to whom he was writing.[1]

In his introductory remarks in his various letters Paul also included certain elements and statements that were unique to the situation. Frequently these unique remarks give us a clue as to his primary reason for writing a particular letter.

Paul's letter to Titus is no exception. His principle concern for the churches in Crete was that they might have a "knowledge of the truth that leads to godliness." In fact, this little New Testament Epistle contains more specific instructions to various groups of people regarding how to live the Christian life than any other. Therefore, it indeed contains a biblical *profile for a Christian life style*. And though a relatively short letter, it is very comprehensive. In reality, it contains all that Christians really need to know in order to determine whether or not they are living a godly life.

A. Paul's Credentials

1. *A servant*

For Paul to identify himself as a "servant" was not new among Christian leaders in the first century. Peter, James, and Jude also identified themselves as "servants of God" or "of Christ" (James 1:1; 2 Peter 1:1; Jude 1).

Paul also used this terminology in his letters to the Romans and the Philippians, although in these Epistles he called himself a "servant of *Jesus Christ*" rather than a "servant of *God*." In doing this he was demonstrating again that he considered God and Christ one. For Paul, to serve Christ was to serve God the Father. And to serve God the Father was to serve the Lord Jesus Christ.

Paul identified himself as a "*servant* [*doulos*] of God," literally, a "bondservant" or a "slave," or one who gives himself up totally to do someone else's will. This, of course, describes Paul's attitude toward his heavenly Father. Following his conversion, he had no other goal for his life but to do the will of God. It was this kind of relationship that set Paul "free"—free to become what God wanted him to be.

This, of course, represents one of those divine mysteries inherent in Christianity. How can a person be a "servant" and yet "free"? There is only one relationship on earth that makes it possible—a relationship with God through Jesus Christ and a relationship with other members of the body of Christ who have experienced the same relationship with God. It is only as a person becomes rightly related to his Creator that he can begin to experience true freedom in his relationships with other people. And the way of freedom comes through servanthood—total commitment to the God of the universe who first became our servant through Jesus Christ (Phil. 2:7).

There is no way to explain this phenomenon adequately. It makes sense, however, when we realize that no one is truly free. By nature, man is a slave to his own selfish nature and to the selfish nature of his fellow men. He is a slave to the law of sin. But in Christ he can be set free from his old nature. And as a member of the body of Christ he has a potential to be set free from the old nature that controls others. He, along with his fellow Christians, can now serve God and others according to the law of love (Gal. 5:13,14).

2. *An apostle*

Paul, when stating his credentials, also called himself "an *apostle* [*apostolos*] of Jesus Christ," which means a delegate or messenger of Christ. As stated earlier, it was a common practice for Paul to identify himself in this way in his letters. And it is clear *why* he identified himself in this way. He wanted others to know that his authority as a messenger of Jesus Christ came directly from God and that he was specifically set apart to communicate the gospel. Consequently, he stated and restated his credentials. Note the following:

Romans 1:1—"Paul, a servant of Christ Jesus, called to *be an apostle* and set apart for the gospel of God. . . ."[2]

1 Corinthians 1:1—"Paul, called to be an *apostle* of Christ Jesus *by the will of God*. . . ."

2 Corinthians 1:1 —"Paul, an *apostle* of Christ Jesus *by the will of God*. . . ."

Galatians 1:1 — "Paul, an *apostle—sent* not from man nor by man, but *by Jesus Christ* and *God the Father*. . . ."

Ephesians 1:1—"Paul, an *apostle* of Christ Jesus *by the will of God*. . . ."

Colossians 1:1—"Paul, an *apostle* of Christ Jesus *by the will of God*. . . ."

1 Timothy 1:1—"Paul, an *apostle* of Christ Jesus *by the command of God* our Savior and of Christ Jesus our hope. . . ."

2 Timothy 1:1—"Paul, an *apostle* of Christ Jesus *by the will of God*, according to the promise of life in Christ Jesus. . . ."

Note also that when Paul wrote to very close friends and missionary companions like Timothy and Titus, he still began his letter with this formal introduction and greeting.

Obviously, they needed no verification of who he was. However, those believers who would hear the letters read and would later have the privilege of reading the letters themselves, *would* need this verification. This is no doubt one reason why Paul was formal, even with his very close companions. And so when he wrote to Titus he said, "Paul, the *servant* of God and an *apostle* of Jesus Christ."

B. Paul's Calling

Paul's *calling* cannot be separated from his *credentials*. This we have already observed from the introductions in his various letters. And this fact is also clear in his letter to Titus. Paul directly related his "servanthood" and "apostleship" to his calling from God to bring people to faith in Jesus Christ and then to lead them to grow in their Christian lives.

1. *Relative to salvation*

Paul identified himself to Titus as "an apostle of Jesus

Christ *for the faith of God's elect*'' (1:1). And a moment later he related this ''faith of God's elect'' to ''the hope of *eternal life,* which God, who does not lie, promised *before the beginning of time*'' (1:2). In other words, Paul was called and commanded to be an apostle to preach the gospel to those God had chosen from eternity so that they might place their faith in the resurrected Christ and be saved. "At his appointed season,'' wrote Paul, ''he brought his word to light through the preaching entrusted to me by the *command* of God our Savior'' (1:3).

The doctrine of election has confused many people. How could God choose people for salvation from before the foundation of the world and still give all men the choice to accept or reject His Son? The fact is that both truths are taught in the Bible. There is no way, humanly speaking, to resolve the tension between them. The tension exists because we are finite and God is infinite. In eternity we will immediately have a much clearer understanding of this concept. It is also possible that we may spend eternity learning more and more how these truths are interrelated.

There are reasons why this doctrine confuses people. It is primarily because election is presented in a nonbiblical way. Though it is a wonderful truth that is definitely taught in Scripture, yet, when compared with the great bulk of New Testament ideas, there is relatively little said about it in the New Testament. But when it *is* presented, one of the basic purposes the New Testament writers had in mind was to provide believers with a sense of security and hope (see Rom. 8; Eph. 1; 1 Peter 1). In Romans 9, Paul was discussing God's dealings with nations and was warning against pride and arrogance.

A true test for any Bible teacher as to whether or not he is communicating this doctrine appropriately or inappropriately is whether or not he is achieving the results the New Testament writers had in mind. If it is taught in a biblical fashion, this great truth will create a sense of security, well-being, humility, and human responsibility. If it is taught inappropriately, it will create insecurity (often reflected in emotional and intellectual confusion), pride (often reflected in an argumentative spirit), and a lack of human responsibility (often reflected in little or no effort in evangelism and missions),

In writing to Titus, Paul took his more frequent approach to the subject of election. He briefly related it to his own calling and sense of human responsibility and then proceeded to instruct Titus regarding every Christian's responsibility to live the Christian life. The apostle Paul, of all New Testament writers, believed and taught the doctrine of election, but of all New Testament Christians, he also demonstrated the greatest sense of concern in preaching the gospel to unbelievers and helping Christians grow spiritually. Human responsibility in spiritual growth is what Paul's letter to Titus is all about.

2. *Relative to sanctification*

Paul identified himself as an "apostle of Jesus Christ for the faith of God's elect and *the knowledge of the truth that leads to godliness*" (1:1).

In some respects we are being unfair to Paul when we separate the experience of salvation from the process of sanctification. Paul's calling and God-ordained task involved both responsibilities; that is, communicating God's eternal truth that leads to both conversion and spiritual growth. Paul was desperately concerned that once a person was saved by faith, he should also grow in the knowledge and grace of Jesus Christ. In fact, this is Paul's primary concern in his letter to Titus—to present "truth that leads to godliness." To help believers "*love* what is good" (1:8), "*teach* what is good" (2:3), and "*do* what is good" (2:7,14; 3:8; 3:14) stands out boldly as a theme in this Epistle.

A TWENTIETH-CENTURY APPLICATION

The apostle Paul was both a *servant* of God and an *apostle* of Jesus Christ. As a servant, his one desire was to do the will of God. And as an apostle, he was under orders to carry out the will of God in preaching the gospel, particularly to the

Gentiles, and to help his converts live lives that reflected godliness. To what extent do Christians today have the same responsibility?

A. What About Apostles Today?

An apostle in New Testament days was a special person, called by God and especially gifted to help launch the church of Jesus Christ. Along with the New Testament prophets, the apostles had a foundational ministry (Eph. 3:20). They were eyewitnesses of Jesus Christ and received their calling and commands directly from Him.

Paul was one of these men. Though his calling came after Christ returned to heaven (Acts 9:1-16), he was still a bona fide apostle and recognized as such by other New Testament believers (Gal. 1:18-24; 2:6-10).

Today there are no apostles, at least not in a New Testament sense. However, their basic function is still applicable to all believers today. Though we do not receive direct revelations from God as they did, we have at our disposal the revelation they received, which is recorded for us in the Bible. And the *command* given to all of us in the Word of God is to *communicate* their message—God's message—to all mankind. This, of course, is what the Great Commission is all about (Matt. 28:19,20). And this is what Paul had in mind when he told Timothy, "And the things you have heard me say in the presence of many witnesses entrust to reliable men who will also be qualified to teach others" (2 Tim. 2:2).

God's will is that the process begun by the apostles go on and be repeated through believers everywhere. Though our involvement in world evangelism and edification may be more limited, none of us is exempt from being a part of this great process. Not all will go to the ends of the earth as God's emissaries, yet we are all to have a part in sharing Christ where we are, sending those who desire to go to the regions beyond, and praying for God's blessing upon them.

B. Are All Christians to Be Servants of God?

Though Paul may have been a special kind of "servant of

God'' because of his apostleship, nothing could be clearer in Scripture than the fact that God's will for *all* believers of *all* time is that they also be His servants. Thus Peter exhorted Christians all over the New Testament world to ''live as servants of God'' (1 Peter 2:16).

A Christian who lives as a servant of God desires to do the will of God in all respects. He wants to conform his life, not to the world's system, but to Jesus Christ. This is what Paul had in mind when he exhorted the Roman Christians: ''Offer yourselves as living sacrifices, holy and pleasing to God—which is your spiritual worship. Do not conform any longer to the pattern of this world, but be transformed by the renewing of your mind. Then you will be able to test and approve what God's will is—his good, pleasing and perfect will'' (Rom. 12:1,2).

A PERSONAL LIFE RESPONSE

To what extent are you involved in an ''apostolic ministry''? Don't misunderstand. I am not suggesting that you are to strive to be another apostle Paul, another apostle Peter, or another apostle John. Rather, to what extent are you taking seriously the Great Commission? To what extent are you involved in sharing Jesus Christ with those who do not know Him personally? And to what extent are you involved in helping other Christians grow in the grace and knowledge of Jesus Christ? God called men like Paul, Peter, John and other apostles to launch the church, to lay the foundations. What are you doing to further the building process? Remember Paul's words to the Ephesian Christians: ''From him the whole body, joined and held together by every supporting ligament, grows and builds itself up in love, *as each part does its work*'' (Eph. 4:16).

What are *you* contributing to this process? The following questions and evaluation scale will help you isolate areas where you could do more:

	Always				Never
1. I am available to God to share Christ with others.	1	2	3	4	5
2. My life style reflects the life style of Jesus Christ to both Christians and non-Christians.	1	2	3	4	5
3. I do what I can to help other Christians grow spiritually.	1	2	3	4	5
4. I am a servant of Jesus Christ, desiring to do His will in all respects.	1	2	3	4	5

NOTE: If you checked a number of fives, chances are you do not have a realistic view of the Christian life. However, if you checked a number of ones or twos, you have some areas in your life that need special attention.

INDIVIDUAL OR GROUP PROJECT

Study Paul's introduction to his Roman letter, verses 1-6. How does this introduction correlate with the introduction in Paul's letter to Titus? What are the common elements? What does he say in the Roman introduction that elaborates on and expands the concepts in the introduction to Titus?

NOTES

[1]Paul identified himself as an *apostle* in most of his Epistles (cf. also Rom. 1:1; 1 Cor. 1:1; 2 Cor. 1:1; Gal. 1:1; Eph. 1:1; Col. 1:1; 1 Tim. 1:1; and 2 Tim. 1:1). The exceptions are Philippians, 1 and 2 Thessalonians, and Philemon. In these four Epistles he was also writing on behalf of others (specifically Timothy and Titus) who were not apostles in the same sense as Paul.

[2]All italicized words in scriptural statements used in this book are the author's and are used to emphasize and clarify certain ideas and concepts.

Chapter II

Titus—a Man Who Measured Up

SOMETHING TO THINK ABOUT

Using the numbers 1 to 5, list in order of importance the ingredients you feel are most necessary in developing credibility with other people.

________ Being an older person

________ Having pure motives

________ Demonstrating compassion and concern for people

________ Manifesting a positive atitude

________ Standing firm for what is right

A LOOK AT PAUL'S LETTER

Paul's Companion

1:4 To Titus,
my true son in our common faith: —— 1
Grace
and
peace
from God the Father
and
Christ Jesus our Savior. —— 2

Paul's Concern

1:5 The reason I left you in Crete
was that you might straighten out what was left
unfinished —— 1
and
appoint elders in every town,
as I directed you. —— 2

WHAT DID PAUL SAY?

A. Paul's Companion

1. Titus—a spiritual son

2. Grace and peace—a spiritual salutation

B. Paul's Concern

1. The need for godly living

2. The need for godly leaders

WHAT DID PAUL MEAN?

There are some Christians who emerge as strong leaders. Their very attitudes and actions generate confidence on the part of others. They soon stand out as being trustworthy and unusually capable.

Titus was that kind of Christian. In some respects he had strengths that some other well-known New Testament Christians did not have. And it was these strengths that caused Paul to lay on his shoulders some very heavy responsibilities—challenges that many of us would rather not accept.

A. Paul's Companion

1. *Titus—a spiritual son*

It appears that Titus became one of Paul's first missionary companions soon after Paul began in earnest to win Gentiles for Christ. Though we cannot be certain, he may have been one of Paul's first converts from among the Gentiles, thus greeting him in this letter as "my true son in our common faith." And this may also be one reason why he took Titus along when he went to Jerusalem to talk with the other apostles about his special calling to evangelize the Gentiles. Perhaps Titus was "Exhibit A" in demonstrating to his Jewish brothers that the message of the gospel was available to *all* mankind (Gal. 2:1-10).

Titus is mentioned elsewhere in the New Testament in eleven verses of Scripture, several of which tell us some very significant things about this man.

First, though he was evidently a young man, he was mature psychologically as well as spiritually. This seems obvious because of the heavy responsibility with which Paul entrusted him. More is said about Titus in his relationship with the Corinthians than with any other group of believers—outside of the Cretans. In other words, Paul allowed Titus to go to Corinth to minister to Christians who were well known for their carnality. Titus demonstrated his maturity when he was successful in helping them shed many aspects of worldliness (2 Cor. 7:5-15).

It may be that Titus delivered Paul's first letter to the Corinthians—a letter filled with very strong exhortations regarding their sinful behavior. The most serious injunction called upon them to deal with a man in the church who was living in open and flagrant immorality (1 Cor. 5). This would be a very difficult task for anyone. But Titus succeeded, not only as a messenger from Paul, but as Paul's direct representative in dealing with sin. He faced the problem head-on, just as Paul would have done himself.

Second, he was a man with pure motives. Paul was very conscientious about his own inner motives. He avoided any activity that could be interpreted as exploitation of others. Consequently, he would often bend over backwards to avoid any appearance of selfish behavior. At times he even gave up what was rightfully his to avoid criticism (1 Cor. 9:1-18).

Titus was a man who thought and acted with the same spirit as Paul and proved to be of great help to him. When Titus had completed his task in Corinth, it was obvious that his motives and behavior were above reproach. Thus Paul could say, "Did we [Titus and I] not act in the same spirit and follow the same course?" (2 Cor. 12:18). This is an obvious reference to the fact that Titus's behavior in Corinth matched that of the apostle Paul himself.

Third, Titus was a man with compassion and concern for people. Paul paid tribute to this quality in Titus when he wrote to the Corinthians, "I thank God, who put into the heart of Titus the same *concern* I have for you" (2 Cor. 8:16). To be equated with Paul in the area of concern and compassion is no doubt the highest tribute any man could receive. Paul would never have made a public statement of this nature had there been any question in his mind regarding Titus's character. Titus had his total confidence.

Fourth, Titus was a man who maintained a positive attitude. When Paul needed a man to confront the Corinthians, Titus voluntarily accepted the challenge. Thus Paul wrote, "Titus not only welcomed our appeal, but he is coming to you with much *enthusiasm* and on his *own initiative*" (2 Cor. 8:17).

Titus was a self-starter. And he thrived on difficult assignments. He did not run away from opportunities—difficult though they may have been—to serve the Lord Jesus Christ. This he proved beyond a shadow of a doubt when he accepted the challenge to visit the Corinthian church. Anyone with lesser stature would have gladly given the "opportunity" to someone else.

Fifth, Titus stood firm for what was right. When Titus arrived in Corinth, he faced a number of people who were highly critical of Paul. They had judged him severely and falsely, questioning his motives and classifying him as a weak person. How easy it would have been for Titus to side with them in their criticisms in order to be accepted and to demonstrate his own strengths.

But not Titus! He interpreted Paul as he was—a man of the highest motives and integrity. Consequently, we can understand Paul's words in his second letter to the Corinthians when he wrote, "God, who comforts the downcast, comforted us by *the coming of Titus*, and not only by his coming but also by the comfort you have given him. He told us," continued Paul, "about your affection, your deep sorrow, *your ardent concern for me*, so that my joy was greater than ever" (2 Cor. 7:6,7).

Thus we can also understand why Paul had such great confidence in Titus. He was loyal—not for loyalty's sake, but because it was the right thing to do. He stood for the truth, no matter what it cost him personally. Furthermore, he did not succumb to the temptation to enhance his own image with the Corinthians by joining them in their criticisms against Paul. And this, of course, is a basic reason why Paul left Titus in Crete to face some church problems that were in some respects even more severe than those in Corinth.

2. *Grace and peace—a spiritual greeting*

As in all his correspondence, Paul used two words to extend his special greetings also to Titus: "*grace* and *peace*." Though these words were common in the New Testament world and were often used in formal correspondence, Paul always used them in the context of Christian theology. Therefore, his greeting included "grace and peace from *God the Father* and *Christ Jesus our Savior*" (1:4). Paul was referring to God's unmerited favor and abounding grace toward mankind when He sent Jesus Christ to be the Savior of the world. He was also referring to the peace with God that all men have when they receive God's gift of eternal life.

B. Paul's Concern

Paul had a deep concern for the Christians in Crete. They were like sheep without a shepherd. In fact, as we will see, there were many false teachers who were leading them astray.

We are not sure when Paul visited the island of Crete. Since Luke does not record any such event in the book of Acts, we can only speculate that Paul must have been released from prison for a time and, before he returned to prison, visited this island, preaching the gospel and securing a number of converts to Christianity.

It also appears that Titus had been with Paul on this preaching mission. Then when Paul had to move on to another location, he left Titus in Crete to help establish the various churches.

Why then this formal letter? There seems to be at least two reasons. First, it was a means of officially supporting Titus in his task. Titus needed the authority of Paul behind his activities. Thus Paul wrote out clearly *why* he had left him in Crete and *what* he was to do. If there were any questions raised by any of the believers regarding the official nature of Titus's responsibility, this letter was available for anyone to read.

A second reason may have been to elaborate on what Paul originally had asked Titus to do. In other words, he wanted to make sure Titus had sufficient information to do the job properly. Thus Paul outlined once again what his concern was for the Cretan Christians.

1. *A need for godly living*

"The reason I left you in Crete," wrote Paul, "was that

you might *straighten out* what was left unfinished . . ." (1:5a).

Paul's first concern related to the general life style of the Cretan Christians. Many expositors interpret this as a directive to organize churches—especially since Paul followed this initial injunction with a reference to appoint elders. Obviously, organization is involved, but there appears to be a deeper meaning behind Paul's concern. What desperately needed "straightening out" was their life style. Being relatively new believers, they had received very little instruction regarding how to live the Christian life. Furthermore, like the Corinthians, they were so ingrained in ungodly and pagan living that it took time to move them toward maturity. Furthermore, to complicate the situation, false teachers were already leading them in the wrong direction. And the life style of these false teachers was anything but godly. Thus Paul instructed Titus regarding the best way to counteract this negative influence.

2. *A need for godly leaders*

"The reason I left you in Crete was that you might *straighten out* what was left unfinished and *appoint elders* in every town, as I directed you" (1:5).

These new and immature Christians needed positive models of Christlike behavior to counteract the negative models of worldliness that the false teachers were. Thus Paul instructed Titus to "appoint elders in every town." Evidently Paul had already directed Titus to care for this matter before he left Crete, but he wanted to make sure that Titus (and all the other Christians in Crete) knew exactly how to select the men who were qualified. In our next three chapters we will see in detail what was expected of a man who was appointed as an elder.

A TWENTIETH-CENTURY APPLICATION

Today the church of Jesus Christ desperately needs men and women to emerge as mature Christians. A man like Titus serves as a dynamic example and model for us all. How can *you* become this kind of person?

1. *Even though you may be young, work hard at becoming psychologically and spiritually mature.* This kind of life style is not automatic. It takes effort. It means eliminating bad habits and establishing good ones. It means being open to correction. It involves having a teachable spirit. You must become a serious student of the Scriptures, learning God's Word and what His will is for your life. You must become a functioning part of the body of Christ, learning to relate to others in unselfish ways.

2. *Keep your motives pure.* Look for opportunities but never be an opportunist. Serve others out of love and concern for them, not for personal gain and advantage. Don't misunderstand. No one can serve others in this way without benefiting personally. Enjoy those benefits when they come. But never allow yourself to reverse that process. To serve for personal gain soon rings hollow, and most thinking people read it loud and clear. People soon avoid those who have selfish motives.

3. *Develop compassion and concern for people.* Again, this is not automatic. You must determine to keep your eyes off yourself and on others. You must stop putting all your energy into meeting your own needs and begin to meet the needs of others. To love people at the feeling level, you must get to know them personally—their joys, their sorrows, their hurts, and their difficulties. You must develop the perspective of Jesus Christ who came to seek and save those who were lost and to give them life abundantly.

4. *Develop a positive attitude.* Like Titus, become a self-starter. Look for opportunities that will strengthen you, challenge you, and help you develop your skills and ability. This, of course, is difficult, especially for the person who has a negative mind-set. But you can reverse that mentality. Begin to think positive thoughts about God's work, about other Christians, and about the opportunities that will enable you to serve the Lord and others.

5. *Always stand firm for what is right.* A temptation we all face is the temptation to compromise our convictions in order to be accepted by others. Be teachable and open to correction, but never compromise in such a way that you violate God's will. And remember, there are ways to disagree without being disagreeable.

   NOTE: If you are not sure about God's will in a particular matter, before responding with a decision, seek advice from other mature Christians.

A PERSONAL LIFE RESPONSE

Check yourself! Where are you in the process of developing the kind of reputation Titus had? To do this, sit down with a mature Christian friend you trust and read through the twentieth-century application. Ask that Christian to give you feedback regarding areas of strength and weakness in your life. Then set up goals in the areas where you need to improve.

NOTE: This kind of project is always threatening, but in the end it is intensely rewarding. The first thing you will gain is respect from your friends.

A PERSONAL OR GROUP PROJECT

Compare Timothy's life with that of Titus. Study the following Scriptures and then contrast the two personalities. Can you discern areas of weakness in Timothy that made him more vulnerable than Titus?

Acts 16:1-5
Philippians 2:19-24
1 Timothy 4:12
1 Timothy 5:23
2 Timothy 1:3-8
2 Timothy 2:1

Chapter III

Needed—Christlike Family Models

SOMETHING TO THINK ABOUT

Do you "agree" or "disagree" with the following statement?

> The "measure of a family" is in most instances the "measure of a man." Why or why not?

A LOOK AT PAUL'S LETTER

An Elder—Who Is He?

1:6 An elder (see related Scriptures for subpoints 1, 2, 3)

An Elder—His Basic Qualifications

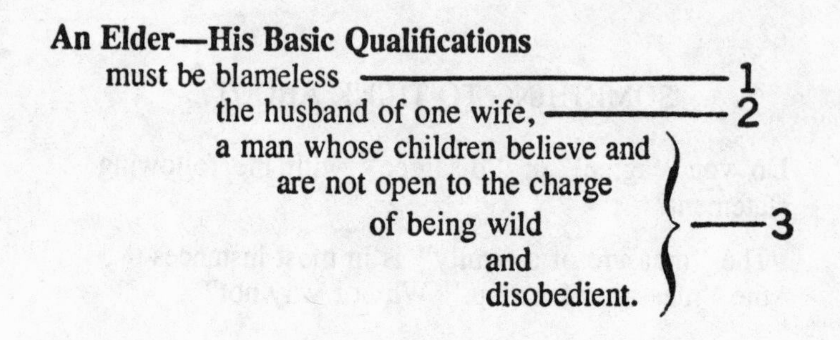

WHAT DID PAUL SAY?

A. An Elder—Who Is He?

1. An elder is to be a shepherd or a pastor
2. An elder is to be a teacher
3. An elder is to be a manager

B. An Elder—Basic Qualifications

1. Being blameless
2. Being the husband of one wife
3. Having a well-managed household

WHAT DID PAUL MEAN?

Paul's basic strategy for solving the life-style problem in Crete may be surprising, especially in view of the way we often try to solve problems in the twentieth-century church. The typical approach today usually involves a series of high-powered sermons to give God's viewpoint on sin. And, of course, we must quickly acknowledge that this method is not wrong. In fact, it may be necessary and proper.

But there is a step that is far more basic than using the verbal approach. Paul demonstrates that step graphically when dealing with the sin problem in Crete. How was Titus to "straighten out what was left unfinished"? That is, how was he to bring people's lives into proper alignment with God's expectations?

Step number one, Paul wrote, was "to appoint elders in every town"—to appoint men who would serve as models of Christlike behavior.

There were many self-imposed leaders in Crete who were anything but godly in their life style. Their attitudes and actions were having a strongly negative influence on many believers. In fact, as we will see later, they were actually "ruining whole households" (1:11). Consequently, in order to counteract this negative influence, Paul's initial strategy called for the appointment of leaders whose own households were in order, whose family life styles would serve as Christlike models in every Christian community.

A. An Elder—Who Is He?

When looking specifically at what should characterize an elder's life style, it is important to understand his role. The Bible clearly teaches that he had at least three basic functions in the New Testament church. Though they are overlapping and interrelated functions, they can be described individually as well.

1. *An elder is to be a shepherd or a pastor*

Paul made this clear when he met with the Ephesian elders

at Miletus. "Guard yourselves," warned Paul, "and *all the flock*. . . . Be *shepherds* of the church of God" (Acts 20:17,28). Peter, too, emphasized this function when he wrote, "To the elders among you, I appeal as a fellow elder. . . . Be *shepherds* of God's flock that is under your care" (1 Peter 5:1,2).

An elder, then, is to care for God's people just as a faithful shepherd cares for his sheep—guarding them, protecting them, and feeding them. In Crete, many believers were like sheep among wolves. False teachers were everywhere, scattering the sheep and destroying the work that Paul and Titus had so faithfully established. Paul's answer to the problem was to appoint elders in every city who could shepherd these believers.

2. *An elder is to be a teacher*

Paul, when writing to Timothy about the appointment of elders, specifically required that an elder be "able to teach" (1 Tim. 3:2). And in his second letter to Timothy, Paul clearly defined what he had in mind with this requirement: "And the Lord's servant must not quarrel; instead, he must be kind to everyone, *able to teach,* not resentful. Those who oppose him he must *gently instruct,* in the hope that God will give them a change of heart and lead them to a *knowledge of the truth*" (2 Tim. 2:24,25).

An elder is responsible to communicate God's truth to Christians. This is why Paul also wrote to Titus, specifying that an elder "must hold firmly to the *trustworthy message* as it has been *taught,* so that he can encourage others by *sound doctrine* and *refute those who oppose it*" (Titus 1:9).

Paul, in writing to Titus, delineated *what* must be done. When he wrote to Timothy, he clearly spelled out *how* it was to be done. But in both passages one thing is clear—it must be done! An elder is to teach God's Word.

3. *An elder is to be a manager*

Again it must be pointed out that these three functions (pastoring, teaching, and managing) are overlapping and interrelated roles. But each is also a unique function. *Pastoring* illustrates guidance and protection. *Teaching* involves nurturing and feeding. And *managing* is more inclusive, encompassing all facets of the ministry. This is quite obvious from Paul's statement in his first letter to Timothy: "The elders who direct [or manage] the affairs of the church well are worthy of double honor, especially those whose work is preaching and teaching" (1 Tim. 5:17). Here Paul includes "teaching" as a distinct part of the process of "managing" or "ruling."

One additional observation about being New Testament leaders. Nowhere does the Bible refer to an individual elder as being in charge of a local church. Rather, the New Testament speaks of the *elders* of a church. Plurality of leadership was the norm in the New Testament. True, there were elders who were paid for carrying out their responsibilities. These were the men who were "worthy of double honor" (1 Tim. 5:17), which simply means they were remunerated because they spent more time in ministering than in other jobs. But this in no way gave them more authority than those who were not paid. Nowhere does the Bible teach the "one-man ministry" as it is so frequently practiced today.

Practically speaking, however, this concept needs some elaboration. The very nature of leadership and how it functions calls for some *one* person to be responsible for coordinating the overall ministry of the church. The Bible does not spell out in detail how this should be carried out in individual local churches at the elder level, but it does illustrate the principle. In the Old Testament people like Moses, Joshua, Samuel, Deborah, David, and Nehemiah stand out clearly as dynamic leaders. In the New Testament we see Jesus Christ Himself, who is designated as the Chief Shepherd (1 Peter 5:4). He was followed by Peter, Paul, Timothy, and Titus, who were particularly involved in the church-planting process. Peter and Paul were apostles who were basically responsible for evangelism and church planting. Timothy and Titus were New Testament pastor-teachers who helped establish local churches until certain men were nurtured and eventually appointed as elders (plural) to take over the ministry of a particular local church.

But note that even in the church-planting process we can observe the multiple-leadership principle at work. Frequently Luke describes the ministry of "Peter *and* John," "Paul *and* Barnabas," and later "Paul *and* Timothy," or "Paul, Silas *and* Timothy." True, Peter and Paul emerge as being primarily responsible for leading these New Testament "teams," but even as men having apostolic authority, they still functioned as individual members of the body of Christ who were responsible to other members of Christ's body. Though they laid the "foundations" of the church, with "Christ Jesus himself as the chief cornerstone," it is clear that in Christ the "whole building is *joined together* and rises to become a holy temple in the Lord" (Eph. 2:19-22).

It is true that though the Bible teaches multiple leadership, it illustrates and experience verifies that one person will usually need to be recognized and appointed as the leader of the team. But this does not mean that he has more authority than the other elders—just more delegated responsibility.

Let me illustrate. For several years I have served as "Senior Staff Pastor" at Fellowship Bible Church in Dallas, Texas. Though recognized as an elder "worthy of double honor" (1 Tim. 5:17-18), that is, a person who has been financially remunerated because of my efforts, I do not classify myself as *the* pastor or *the* elder of the church. Rather, I am one among equals. True, I have had more *delegated responsibility,* but it does not mean I have more *authority* than the other elders. Their words, ideas, and opinions are just as important as mine. I am responsible to them and we are all responsible to each other. In fact, the Scriptures teach that those of us who are recognized as key leaders in the church are really greater servants. Even Christ, the Lord of the universe, recognized this principle at work in His own life when He said that the one who was *greatest* was the *one who serves* (Luke 22:24-17).

Multiple leadership in the church, then, is by design. God's will is that there be more than one man and his family serving as godly models to other believers. The more Christlike family units there are, the greater visual impact and example on other members of the body of Christ—and the world. And this leads us to what Paul believed was the most basic qualification for an elder.

B. An Elder—Basic Qualifications

1. *Being blameless*

Paul begins his list of qualifications for an elder with an overarching characteristic—to "be blameless." Obviously, he was not referring to "perfection," for no man on this earth, apart from Jesus Christ, has lived a perfect life. Rather, Paul was talking about having a "good reputation," or being "above reproach."

Timothy stands out as a vivid illustration of this quality. When Paul came to Lystra just prior to beginning his second missionary journey, a number of the Christian brothers were talking about a dynamic young man named Timothy. To be specific, Luke records that believers from Lystra and Iconium "spoke well of him" (Acts 16:2). In other words, Timothy had a good reputation as a Christian. He was "blameless" in the eyes of those making up the Christian community. There were no specific flaws in his Christian life style that would bring reproach to the cause of Jesus Christ. Consequently, Paul invited Timothy to be his missionary companion, and this resulted in a deep and abiding relationship and ministry.

As we have already observed in a previous chapter, Titus was also this kind of man. He was mature both spiritually and psychologically, maintaining pure motives, evidencing compassion and concern for people, demonstrating a positive attitude toward the ministry, and always standing firm for what was right. There is no better way to develop a good reputation both in the Christian and the non-Christian world. This quality made Titus trustworthy, and it goes without saying that only a man "who measures up" in trustworthiness is eligible to select and appoint others as elders. Of course, both Titus and Timothy qualified.

2. *Being the husband of one wife*

How does a Christian—particularly a married Christian with a family—develop a good reputation? Paul zeros in on two foundational characteristics. The first is to be "a husband of one wife."

There is considerable discussion among evangelical Christians as to what Paul meant by this qualification. Actually, the original language in its most general meaning simply refers to "a one-woman man." There is a certain grammatical ambiguity that must be interpreted contextually.

Personally, I believe Paul was saying that a man who serves as an elder in a church must be sexually related to only one woman. Since it was relatively common for men in the first-century world to have more than one woman in their lives beside their legal wives, Paul had to deal with this issue specifically. Though this kind of life style is also reflective of the twentieth-century world, it was an even more open and accepted practice in the first century. Married men often visited and supported temple prostitutes on a regular basis as well as using slave girls to satisfy their sexual desires. Paul, then is dealing with moral purity. If married, a man who aspires to leadership in the church *must* be loyal to his wife, having no other woman for his sexual interests.

Obviously, this loyalty is a quality of maturity that all Christians must attain to. In fact, nearly every New Testament Epistle deals with premarital and marital sexual sins and warns against them. By their very calling, Christians are to live above the standards of the world in the area of sexual ethics. In order to be mature spiritually, one may allow no compromise in this area of life.

3. *Having a well-managed household*

The second foundational qualification that builds the elder's reputation in the community is a well-ordered home. Paul wrote to Titus that an elder must be "a man whose children believe and are not open to the charge of being wild and disobedient" (Titus 1:6). To Timothy, he put it another way: "He must manage his own family well and see that his children obey him with proper respect" (1 Tim. 3:4).

Again, many Christians have wrestled with trying to determine what Paul had in mind with this qualification. Does this mean a man should not serve as an elder if he isn't married? If it did, it would be very strange for Paul, who perhaps had never married, to set up this qualification for eldership. Furthermore, we have little evidence that either Timothy or Titus were married. What Paul seems to be saying is that the behavior of a man's children who are of age is a significant reflection of his maturity and capability as a leader. Since marriage and family life is a normal state for most men, Paul treats this as a basic qualification. He by no means excludes those mature men who may have chosen a single life style or because of various circumstances are yet unmarried.

Furthermore, Paul is not saying that a man and wife with no children or with young children who are not of a believing age are disqualified. Again, he is dealing with a general and all-inclusive qualification. In essence, he is saying that if a man is married and has children who are of age, they should be Christians who are not living in open rebellion against God.

It is also important to understand cultural patterns in interpreting what Paul is saying in applying this principle to the twentieth-century church. In the New Testament world, the extended family was normal. Grown and married children often lived under the same roof and were still responsible to follow the leadership of the father (or grandfather). A household of this nature that was not in order—a household whose adult children were "wild and disobedient"—was certainly a reflection of a man's inability to manage those closest to him. Thus Paul asks, "If anyone does not know how to manage his own family, how can he take care of God's church?" (1 Tim. 3:5).

This raises even more specific questions. Does this mean a man should not function as an elder if one of his children strays away from the Lord and violates God's standards? There is no simple answer to this question. A simple "yes" or "no" will not suffice. Paul's statement regarding this qualification in both 1 Timothy and Titus must be interpreted in context. Remember that he is dealing with a man's reputation. And the most basic ingredient that demonstrates maturity is in the area of family life. Is he a man who is morally pure? Is his family in order? In other words, what is the overall image of this man's household in the local community? If there are specific family problems that cause a decided lack of respect and confidence in this person on the part of both Christians and non-Christians, it seems quite obvious that it would be better for a man not to serve as a spiritual leader in the church, but rather concentrate his efforts on getting his priorities straight and in putting his family life together. If, on the other hand, the problems are not public and if they are in the process of being solved in a particular community affecting a man's reputation, I personally believe this person can serve as an elder, providing he measures up to the other biblical requirements for the office. Remember that just as there is no perfect individual, there is no perfect family. And in every family there will be periods of stress resulting in periodic straying from the "straight and narrow." The important thing is that in the eyes of others there is steady, overall progress toward maturity. How a wife and children relate to a husband and father is indeed a very important reflection of Christian maturity or lack of it.

Paul no doubt referred to family life first in demonstrating a good reputation in order to point out the contrast with the households of false teachers who were already at work in Crete leading Christians astray. In a future chapter, it will become clear that these men certainly did not measure up to Paul's most basic qualification. There was no way their families could be in order.

A TWENTIETH-CENTURY APPLICATION

It's true. The measure of a family is indeed the measure of a man—and a woman! What we need today in the twentieth-century church, as the Christians did in Crete, are more Christlike family models. This is especially true in a society where family life is deteriorating rapidly. In some parts of our country there are now more divorces than marriages.

How can we strengthen the home, and consequently, strengthen the church, which will inevitably affect society, at least in the community in which we live and worship? Paul's injunctions are just as relevant today as they were two thousand years ago.

1. *Moral purity*. Today's moral value system is changing rapidly. Though we have not reached the depths to which the Greek and Roman cultures fell, we are rapidly moving in that direction. The influence of literature, movies, and television are all contributing to and reflecting the moral decadence that is all about us.

   What about your own life? Are you—as a husband, wife, single person—maintaining a life of purity? Whether married or single, what we sow we will reap. Marital unfaithfulness and sexual promiscuity, whether in mind or body, run counter to God's will for mankind. And a basic answer to creating moral purity in the church is to appoint leaders who are totally committed to God's standard in this area of their lives.

2. *A well-ordered family*. Paul viewed the well-ordered home as a true test of a man's maturity and ability to lead other Christians, especially a home that has passed the test of time. When the whole household is committed to Jesus Christ and the wife is dedicated to her husband and grown children particularly respect and love their father, there is strong evidence that this man is spiritually and pscyhologically mature. He will certainly be able to manage the church of God (1 Tim. 3:5).

   But when this is not true, there may be serious problems in the church if a man is appointed as a spiritual leader. First, the very weakness that made him a poor husband and father will cause him to be a poor leader in the church. Second, if he accepts such a position, his family will have even less respect for him, causing even greater problems in the home. In other words, we can make matters worse for his family by ignoring this important criterion for maturity.

One word of caution! The fact that some grown Christian children go astray from God's will does not always mean a man has not been a good father. The home is not an island. The world's influences are sometimes felt, no matter how effective the Christian environment in the home. Furthermore, once children leave home, Satan can sometimes gain access in ways that do not necessarily reflect on parental effectiveness.

So, be careful! Paul is establishing a general principle. A well-ordered household usually reflects maturity in parents. But a "black sheep" in a family is not always a disqualifying factor by which we may determine that a Christian will not make a good spiritual leader in the church. It is true, however, that if a wayward son or daughter hurts the reputation of the father in a *particular community,* it would be wise for that father not to maintain a prominent position in the church.

3. *A goal for every Christian man.* To be a good husband and father, to have a well-ordered household, should be a goal for every Christian man. All Christian husbands are to love their wives "just as Christ loved the church" (Eph. 5:25). They are to live with them in a considerate way and to show them respect as heirs with them "of the gracious gift of life." Peter goes so far as to say that a man who does not live this way with his wife will experience "hindered" prayer (1 Peter 3:7).

   Furthermore, fathers are not to provoke their children to anger but to "bring them up in the training and instruction of the Lord" (Eph. 6:4). Paul elaborated on this concept with a personal illustration when he said he ministered among the Thessalonians "as a father deals with his own children," as he went about "encouraging, comforting and urging" them (1 Thess. 2:11,12). This illustration, of course, shows how Paul viewed the father's responsibility to the children. He is not just to rear a family, but to encourage, comfort, and urge the individual children in that family, "to live lives worthy of God."

A PERSONAL LIFE RESPONSE

In light of this study, select one area in your family—as a husband, wife, or single person—where you need to grow spiritually. Decide on one basic step you will take immediately to become more mature in this area of your life.

Chapter IV

Needed—Christlike Men

SOMETHING TO THINK ABOUT

Check three of the most important qualities you believe cause a person to have a *bad* reputation:

_____ Overbearing
_____ Quick-tempered
_____ Given to much wine
_____ Violent
_____ Pursuing dishonest gain
_____ Other _______________

Check three of the most important things you believe cause a person to have a *good* reputation:

_____ Loving what is good
_____ Being a self-controlled person
_____ Living a holy life
_____ Living a disciplined life
_____ Other _______________

A LOOK AT PAUL'S LETTER

1:7 Since an overseer is entrusted with God's work,
he must be blameless—

What Causes a Bad Reputation

not overbearing, —— 1
not quick-tempered, —— 2
not given to much wine, —— 3
not violent, —— 4
not pursuing dishonest gain. —— 5

What Causes a Good Reputation

1:8 Rather he must be hospitable, —— 1
one who loves what is good, — 2
who is self-controlled, — 3
upright, —— 4
holy —— 5
and
disciplined. —— 6

WHAT DID PAUL SAY?

A. What Causes a Bad Reputation

1. An overbearing personality
2. Quick-temperedness
3. Being given to much wine
4. Violence
5. Pursuit of dishonest gain

B. What Causes a Good Reputation

1. Being hospitable
2. Loving what is good
3. Being self-controlled
4. Being upright and holy
5. Being holy
6. Being disciplined

WHAT DID PAUL MEAN?

Having a Christlike family and being a Christlike father are certainly inseparable concepts, though it is possible for one to be a Christlike man without being married and having a family. The converse, of course, is seldom true, for as stated in the previous lesson, the "measure of a family" is usually the "measure of a man." In most instances it takes a Christlike man to produce a Christlike family. In my experience I have seen very few exceptions, although I do know of some situations where a godly wife and mother has been able to compensate remarkably well for her husband's failure.

In this letter to Titus Paul assumed that most men who would seek spiritual leadership in the church and be appointed to eldership would be married men who had grown children, who in some instances would already be married themselves, all of them together forming a rather large and extended family unit. Unfortunately, some of the Christian "households" in Crete had already been led astray by spiritually unqualified men (1:11). In some instances the men who led these families astray were probably the fathers themselves. Thus Paul cautioned Timothy to look at the results of the man's life style within his own family unit. For, as Paul wrote to Timothy, if a man could not manage his own family, he certainly was not fit to manage the church of God (1 Tim. 3:5).

After dealing with the most basic qualification for eldership, Paul moved on and very specifically and clearly outlined the qualifications that make a man Christlike and, if married, make him a good husband and father. "Since an overseer [or elder] is entrusted with God's work," he wrote, "he *must* be blameless" (1:7); that is, he must have a good reputation, not only in his family life but also in his personal life.[1]

A. What Causes a Bad Reputation?

Paul first of all presented the concept of being "blameless" or having a "good reputation" from a negative perspective. What causes a man to have a *bad* reputation? He outlined those qualities that should *not* be present in a person's life.

1. *An overbearing personality*

The apostle Peter defines this kind of person very graphically in his second Epistle (2 Peter 2:10). "Overbearing" people are "those who follow the corrupt desire of their sinful natures and despise authority." They are "bold and *arrogant*"—or "self-willed," as the basic word is translated in the New American Standard Bible.

An "overbearing" Christian is a person who is a "law unto himself." He almost always has to have his own way. Others are always wrong! He is always right! He is his own authority.

It is easy to see why this kind of person should not be appointed to spiritual leadership in the church. Just as this kind of man as husband and/or father destroys his own wife and children, so he can very easily destroy the family of God. All it takes is one person with this characteristic to generate disunity in the body of Jesus Christ.

2. *Quick-temperedness*

A "quick-tempered" person easily "flies off the handle" or "loses his cool." He does not deal with the ordinary functions and frustrations of life with emotional stability. He often loses control and "strikes out" at others, if not physically, at least verbally.

A quick-tempered Christian can be devastating to the cause of Christ. Not only is he a bad example and model, but he will inevitably hurt others and stunt their spiritual growth.

Understand that the Bible does not classify *all* anger as sin. Thus Paul wrote to the Ephesians: "In your anger *do not sin:* Do not let the sun go down while you are still angry" (4:26). In other words, Christians should deal with their anger. It should be kept under control. A *quick*-tempered Christian is "out of control."

3. *Being given to much wine*

New Testament Christians were often tempted to revert to their old life style in the matter of drinking. Since wine was a very common beverage with meals, they could very easily overindulge.

A mature Christian should not allow himself to be dominated or controlled by anything that will harm his body, cloud his thinking, or hinder his testimony for Jesus Christ. Thus Paul wrote, "So whether you eat or drink or whatever you do, do it all for the glory of God" (1 Cor. 10:31).

4. *Violence*

To be violent literally means to be a "striker"; that is, a person who physically strikes out at another person. There is, of course, progression in Paul's list of negative characteristics—a person who is "quick-tempered" to begin with can very easily lose *complete* control when he is under the influence of alcohol.

It must be noted however that a "verbally" pugnacious person is certainly as destructive as a person who becomes physically violent. To inflict psychological pain can be even more devastating than to inflict physical pain. Verbal abuse can leave scars in the human personality that are not easily erased.

There is no place for this kind of Christian in the leadership of the church. Rather, as Paul wrote to Timothy, "Don't have anything to do with foolish and stupid arguments, because you know they produce quarrels. And the Lord's servant must not quarrel; instead, he must be kind to everyone, able to teach, not resentful. Those who oppose him he must gently instruct, in the hope that God will give them a change of heart leading them to a knowledge of the truth" (2 Tim. 2:23-25).

5. *Pursuit of dishonest gain*

One of the marks of a false teacher or leader in Crete was his impure motives in regard to material things. Not only were these men "teaching things they ought not to teach," but they were doing it "for the sake of dishonest gain" (Titus 1:11). To counter this problem, Paul directed Titus to appoint spiritual leaders who would *not* pursue dishonest gain.

It is important to note that money in itself is not evil. Neither is it wrong for spiritual leaders to accept money for their work and effort. In fact, Jesus Christ Himself made it clear that "the worker deserves his wages" (Luke 10:7). And Paul specifically taught that "the elders who direct the affairs of the church well are worthy of double honor" (1 Tim. 5:17); that is, elders or pastors who spend much of their time in the ministry, especially in the area of "teaching and preaching" must be remunerated for their work.

However, financial gain is not the primary reason for one to be in the ministry. This is why Peter also instructed elders in the various New Testament churches: "Be shepherds of God's flock that is under your care, serving as overseers—not because you must, but because you are willing, as God wants you to be; *not greedy for money,* but eager to serve" (1 Peter 5:2).

What, then, causes a spiritual leader to have a bad reputation? If he is overbearing, quick-tempered, given to much wine, and violent, and if he pursues dishonest gain, he will bring incredible reproach upon the name of Jesus Christ. Of all people, a man entrusted with God's work should be free from these characteristics.

B. What Causes a Good Reputation?

Paul turned from the negative in verse 7 to the positive in verse 8. After outlining what a spiritual leader *should not* be like, he outlines what he *should* be like.

1. *Being hospitable*

Showing hospitality—sharing material blessings with others—stands out frequently in the Bible as a mark of Christian maturity. It is a reflection of Christlike love (Rom. 12:9-13; Heb. 13:1,2; 1 Peter 4:8,9). Not only is it commanded in Scripture as a spiritual responsibility, but it is frequently illustrated in the lives of New Testament Christians.

This is a particularly important qualification for a spiritual leader in the church. It is the opposite of "pursuing dishonest gain," which is a reflection of selfishness. By contrast, an elder should be willing to use his material possessions, meager though they may be, as a means to minister to others.

2. *Loving what is good*

To "love what is good" means to pursue good rather than evil. In fact, Paul wrote that a mature Christian is to "overcome evil *with* good" (Rom. 12:21). And again Paul wrote that "we are God's workmanship created in Christ Jesus to do *good* works" (Eph. 2:10). This is to be the "normal" Christian life, and our efforts in doing good are to be directed to *all* men—not just to fellow Christians (Gal. 6:10).

An elder is to minister to all kinds and classes of people. True, his primary ministry is to shepherd, teach, and manage the flock of God. But, as with all believers, he is to have a ministry to "all men," attempting to lead "them to a knowledge of the truth, . . . that they will come to their senses and escape from the trap of the devil, who has taken them captive to do his will" (2 Tim. 2:25,26). One of the best ways to achieve this goal is to "love what is good." This is one reason why Paul in his letter to Timothy emphasized the fact that an elder "must also have a good reputation with outsiders" (1 Tim. 3:7).

3. *Being self-controlled*

"Self-control" is an important mark of maturity in a Christian's life and one that Paul was uniquely concerned about, especially in his letter to Titus. In fact, he used the word five times to emphasize the significance of this quality in the lives of *all* Christians (1:8; 2:2,5,6,12).

What is self-control? How is it defined biblically? The word is used to describe a person who is in control of his physical, psychological, and spiritual faculties. English words that are used in various translations to convey the meaning of the original Greek word are *sensible, sober,* and *of a sound mind.* Putting it another way, a self-controlled Christian is not in bondage to fleshly desires, his impulses, and his passions.

Again we see a contrast with the characteristics listed in the previous sections. Obviously, a self-controlled person is not quick-tempered, addicted to wine, or violent.

4. *Being upright and holy*

The next two words Paul used to describe maturity and the

criteria for selecting spiritual leaders are very similar in meaning. In fact, they are synonyms. Both words refer to practical holiness.

Paul, Silas, and Timothy demonstrated this quality in their lives when they served in Thessalonica. Later, when Paul wrote to the church, he said, "You are witnesses, and so is God, of how *holy, righteous* and blameless we were among you who believed" (1 Thess. 2:10).

These three New Testament leaders were living models of Christianity. They desired that the new believers in Thessalonica see the righteousness of Jesus Christ flowing through their lives. And no doubt they achieved this goal, otherwise they could not have written about it and called on God as their witness. This is also why Paul could write to the Corinthians and say, "Follow my example, as I follow the example of Christ" (1 Cor. 11:1).

These qualities more than any others summarize the life of Christ. This is the kind of man He was, even in his humanity. This is what made him a great and acceptable high priest (Heb. 7:26). He demonstrated for us what it means to live "in this world" without being "a part of this world." He is not only our Savior from sin but also our example in living a life that is not dominated by sin. Though He was perfect in everything He did and we are imperfect, yet we are by His grace and strength to emulate His life (Phil. 2:5).

5. *Being disciplined*

Paul illustrated this quality in his first letter to the Corinthians. As he was writing, he raised the question regarding an athletic contest—specifically a foot race: "Do you not know that in a race all the runners run, but only one gets the prize?" Then Paul made the application to the Christian life: "Run in such a way as to get the prize. Everyone who competes in the games goes into *strict training*" (1 Cor. 9:24-25). Here Paul is referring to the same process that he mentioned in Titus 1:8. "Strict training" involves self-discipline. Anyone who participates in an athletic contest must get ready both mentally and physically.

As already mentioned, Paul applied this concept to the

Christian life. It is to be a disciplined life. Thus Paul wrote of himself: "Therefore, I do not run like a man running aimlessly; I do not fight like a man shadow boxing. No, I beat my body and make it my slave so that after I have preached to others, I myself will not be disqualified for the prize" (1 Cor. 9:26-27).

A TWENTIETH-CENTURY APPLICATION

In applying these truths to our lives, we must remember first of all that these qualities are just as relevant to every Christian as they are to those who desire to be spiritual leaders in the church. These characteristics are marks of spiritual maturity for all believers. Paul is simply describing a profile for a Christian life style and those who lead us spiritually should, of all people, be models of what that life style should be.

The following questions are designed to help *every* believer evaluate his life in the light of these biblical criteria:

1. Am I *overbearing?* That is, do I allow my old nature to take control in my relationships with others? For example, do I have to have the last word in every discussion? Do I find it difficult to agree with others? Do I force my opinions on other people? All affirmative answers to these questions are evidences of an overbearing attitude.

   A SCRIPTURE TO THINK ABOUT: "Do nothing out of selfish ambition or vain conceit, but in humility consider others better than yourselves. Each of you should look not only to your own interests, but also to the interests of others" (Phil. 2:3,4).

2. Am I *quick-tempered?* That is, do I easily lose control of my temper? Do I speak before I think? Do I find it difficult to be objective about a situation when I am the object of criticism? Do I hurt people easily? Do people hesitate to ask me about sensitive issues?

   A SCRIPTURE TO THINK ABOUT: "The wisdom that comes from heaven is first of all pure; then peace loving, considerate, submissive, full of mercy and good fruit, impartial and sincere. Peacemakers who sow in peace raise a harvest of righteousness" (James 3:17,18).

3. Am I *addicted* to anything that affects my psychological and physical well being? What about food? What about drink? What about any other oral habits?

   A SCRIPTURE TO THINK ABOUT: "Do you not know that your body is a temple of the Holy Spirit, who is in you, whom you have received from God? You are not your own; you were bought with a price. Therefore honor God with your body" (1 Cor. 6:19,20).

4. Am I a *pugnacious* type of person; that is, do I strike out at others either physically or verbally? Do I ever resort to subtle ways of hurting people, even though it may appear to be a "gentle" approach? For example, do I "gossip" about people under the guise of personal concern?

   A SCRIPTURE TO THINK ABOUT: "The tongue is a small part of the body, but it makes great boasts. Consider what a great forest is set on fire by a small spark. The tongue also is a fire, a world of evil among the parts of the body. It corrupts the whole person, sets the whole course of his life on fire, and is itself set on fire by hell" (James 3:5,6).

5. Do I ever pursue *dishonest gain?* Am I honest in all financial matters? Do I keep accurate records? If an employer, am I fair and honest with my employees? Am I above board with the government?

   A SCRIPTURE TO THINK ABOUT: "Give to everyone what you owe him: If you owe taxes, pay taxes; if revenue, then revenue, if respect, then respect; if honor, then honor. Let no debt remain outstanding, except the continuing debt to love one other, for he who loves his fellow man has fulfilled the law" (Rom. 13:7,8).

6. Am I *hospitable?* Do I use my home as a means of ministering to others? Am I basically unselfish with my material possessions? Do I share my blessings with others?

   A SCRIPTURE TO THINK ABOUT: "Be devoted

to one another in brotherly love. Honor one another above yourselves. Never be lacking in zeal, but keep your spiritual fervor, serving the Lord. Be joyful in hope, patient in affliction, faithful in prayer. Share with God's people who are in need. Practice hospitality'' (Rom. 12:10-13).

7. Do I *love what is good?* What evidence do I have that I am overcoming evil with good? What about my life style in general? Could I write "good" over what I read, what I see, what I listen to, and what I do?

   A SCRIPTURE TO THINK ABOUT: "Finally, brothers, whatever is true, whatever is noble, whatever is right, whatever is pure, whatever is lovely, whatever is admirable—if anything is excellent or praiseworthy—think about such things'' (Phil. 4:8).

8. Am I *self-controlled?* Can I classify myself as being sensible, sober, and having a sound mind?

   A SCRIPTURE TO THINK ABOUT: "For the grace of God that brings salvation has appeared to all men. It teaches us to say 'No' to ungodliness and worldly passions, and to live *self-controlled,* upright and godly lives in this present age'' (Titus 2:11,12).

9. Am I *upright* and *holy?*

   A SCRIPTURE TO THINK ABOUT: "You were taught, with regard to your former way of life, to put off your old self, which is being corrupted by its deceitful desires; to be made new in the attitude of your minds; and to put on the new self, created to be like God in true righteousness and holiness'' (Eph. 4:22-24).

10. Am I disciplined?

    A SCRIPTURE TO THINK ABOUT: "For God did not give us a spirit of timidity, but a spirit of power, of love, and of self-discipline'' (2 Tim. 1:7).

A PERSONAL LIFE RESPONSE

Now that you have looked at these characteristics somewhat in depth, both from a first-century and a twentieth-century perspective, evaluate your own life style. How would you rate yourself in each of these areas?

	Dissatisfied						*Satisfied*
1. Not overbearing	1	2	3	4	5	6	7
2. Not quick-tempered	1	2	3	4	5	6	7
3. Not addicted to wine (or other things)	1	2	3	4	5	6	7
4. Not violent	1	2	3	4	5	6	7
5. Not pursuing dishonest gain	1	2	3	4	5	6	7
6. Hospitable	1	2	3	4	5	6	7
7. Loving what is good	1	2	3	4	5	6	7
8. Self-controlled	1	2	3	4	5	6	7
9. Upright and holy	1	2	3	4	5	6	7
10. Disciplined	1	2	3	4	5	6	7

NOTES

[1]The words *overseer* (or *bishop*) and *elder* are used by Paul as interchangeable concepts. In fact, he used both titles within the space of two verses in this letter to Titus. When writing to a church that was made up exclusively of Jewish believers, Paul used the word *elder*. When writing to a church that was made up of both Jew and Gentile converts, he often used the word *bishop* or *overseer*. Jewish believers understood clearly the concept of "eldership" in that this was a common title used to describe leaders in Israel. Converts out of the pagan Greek and Roman culture clearly understood the word to describe leaders in their social system. In both instances Paul took a common title and gave the word a new meaning in order to describe a new function.

Chapter V

Needed—a Trustworthy Message

SOMETHING TO THINK ABOUT

Check the statements that best describe your attitude toward the message of the Bible:

- ☐ There is little historical evidence to support the message of the Bible.
- ☐ The Bible is a book of myths and interesting stories that teach definite spiritual truths, but it cannot be classified as God's revealed Word.
- ☐ I don't believe the Bible is completely trustworthy, but I believe it anyway.
- ☐ I believe the message of the Bible is completely trustworthy.

A LOOK AT PAUL'S LETTER

The Message—Why Was It Trustworthy?

1:9 He [an overseer]

must hold firmly ——— B1
to the trustworthy message

as it has been taught,

The Message—the Overseer's Response in Attitude and Actions

so that he can encourage others by sound doctrine —2
and
refute those who oppose it. ——— 3

WHAT DID PAUL SAY?

A. The Message—Why Was It Trustworthy?

1. Because of what Christ taught
2. Because of what Christ's disciples taught
3. Because of God's verification through supernatural phenomena

(These subpoints developed from related Scripture)

B. The Message—the Overseer's Response in Attitude and Actions

1. Hold firmly to it
2. Encourage others with it
3. Refute those who oppose it

WHAT DID PAUL MEAN?

To this point Paul had carefully and specifically outlined for Titus what should characterize both an elder's family life and his personal life (Titus 1:6-8). He then culminated the list of qualifications by describing what a spiritual leader's attitudes and actions should be toward the Word of God. "He must hold firmly to the trustworthy message as it has been taught," wrote Paul, "so that he can encourage others by sound doctrine and refute those who oppose it" (Titus 1:9).

A. The Message—Why Was It Trustworthy?

Paul used a very important word in this verse to describe the content of Christianity. He called it *trustworthy*—a word meaning reliable, dependable, faithful. In other words, we can trust what God has said; and even more significant, we can be sure God has said it.

This leads to a very important question. How could New Testament Christians be sure that what they were teaching and being taught was indeed the Word of God? As Paul wrote to Titus, he assumed the answer to this question since this young pastor was well-informed regarding "sound doctrine." No explanation was needed. Titus knew very well what Paul was referring to. He had heard this message taught many times, not only by Paul but also by other New Testament leaders. This is why Paul had left him in Crete to establish the churches. He both exemplified in his own life the message of Christianity and was well-informed theologically. In fact, Titus had been in Jerusalem when Paul was confirmed as an apostle by Peter, James, and John. He had no doubt listened intently to these men as they compared notes in their understanding of the message of Christianity. It was then that the men who had been taught directly by Jesus Christ for three and one-half years confirmed that the message Paul had received from Christ after He went back to heaven was in essence the same message they had heard from Him as He walked on earth (Gal. 2:1-10).

How then did New Testament Christians know what the

true message of Christianity was and why it was trustworthy? The author of the Hebrew letter outlines very succinctly but very profoundly the answer to this question.[1]

1. *Because of what Christ taught*

The most important and basic reason why the message of Christianity is clear and trustworthy relates to the One who is the Essence of Christianity—Jesus Christ Himself.

In outlining the reasons why the message of Christianity is reliable and trustworthy, the author of Hebrews begins with the very message Jesus taught while on earth. He reminds us that this message of salvation "was first announced by the Lord" (Heb. 2:3).

In previous centuries, God had spoken to mankind through the prophets in the Old Testament, but "in these last days he has spoken to us by his Son, whom he appointed heir of all things, and through whom he made the universe" (Heb. 1:2). Jesus Christ came into this world, was born as a human being in Bethlehem of Judea, grew up in a little town called Nazareth, and at the age of thirty began a public ministry. He went everywhere throughout His native land teaching who He was and why He had come into the world. His primary message can be summarized with the words He spoke to Thomas: "I am the way—and the truth and the life. No one comes to the Father except through me" (John 14:6).

C. S. Lewis, who was once an agnostic and a professor at Cambridge, made a very logical statement following his own conversion to Jesus Christ. In *Mere Christianity* he wrote:

> I am trying here to prevent anyone saying the really foolish thing that people often say about Him: "I'm ready to accept Jesus as a great moral teacher, but I don't accept His claim to be God." That is the one thing we must not say. A man who is merely a man and says the sort of things that Jesus said would not be a great moral teacher. He would either be a lunatic—on a level with a man who says he is a poached egg—or else he would be the devil of Hell. You must make your choice. Either this man was, and is, the Son of God: or else a madman or something worse.[2]

New Testament Christians who walked and talked with Jesus knew beyond a shadow of a doubt what He taught about Himself. There was no question in their minds. So committed were they to His claims that many died for their convictions. And this leads us to the second reason the Hebrew author gave as evidence that the message of Christianity was trustworthy.

2. *Because of what Christ's disciples taught*

Not only was the message of salvation "first announced by the Lord" but it was also "confirmed to us by those who heard him" (Heb. 2:3). One of Jesus' first actions was to select twelve men who would be with Him for the three and one-half years He ministered on earth. In large part they were aware of His every attitude and action. Where He went, so did they. What he taught, they heard. What He did, they saw. Thus John, one of the twelve apostles, wrote, "That which was from the beginning, which we have heard, which we have seen with our eyes, which we have looked at and our hands have touched—this we proclaim concerning the Word of Life. The life appeared; we have seen it and testify to it, and we proclaim to you the eternal life, which was with the Father and has appeared to us. We proclaim to you what we have seen and heard, so that you also may have fellowship with us. And our fellowship is with the Father and with his Son, Jesus Christ" (1 John 1:1-3).

So convinced were these men that Jesus Christ was who He said He was that they were indeed willing to lay down their lives to communicate this message to others. And most of them did. Even Judas, who turned against Christ, acknowledged just before he committed suicide that he had "betrayed innocent blood" (Matt. 27:4).

The twelve apostles, of course, represent only a small segment of those who heard Jesus' message and who witnessed His miraculous life. Paul, writing to the Corinthians, first summarized the "trustworthy message" and then referred to those who had witnessed these things: "For what I received I passed on to you as of first importance: that Christ died for our sins according to the Scriptures, that He was buried, that He was raised on the third day according to the Scriptures, and that He appeared to Peter, and then to the Twelve. After that, he appeared to more than *five hundred* of the brothers at the same time, most of whom are still living, though some have fallen asleep. Then he appeared to James, then to all the apostles, and last of all he appeared to me also, as to one abnormally born" (1 Cor. 15:3-8).

The trustworthy Christian message involved Christ's birth, life, death, resurrection, and ascension. So many were the witnesses to these events that only the totally ignorant can rationally deny them.

What Christ taught and what those who heard Him had to say about Him provided the New Testament world with a great reservoir of consistent Christian truth. There was no doubt as to the trustworthiness of the message on which Christianity was built. However, God went farther—much farther—to make sure people *really* knew and understood that this message was indeed trustworthy. This we see outlined by the author of Hebrews as the third reason.

3. *Because of God's verification through supernatural phenomena*

We've looked at two reasons why we should never "drift away" from God's message. First, it was "announced by the Lord." Second, it was "confirmed to us by those who heard him." The third reason was perhaps most important in causing New Testament believers to accept Christ's message as true and trustworthy: "God also testified to it by signs, wonders and various miracles, and gifts of the Holy Spirit distributed according to his will" (Heb. 2:4).

All of the words used to describe God's phenomenal verification of His message to mankind (signs, wonders, miracles, gifts) were very similar and interrelated concepts. All represent God's supernatural power. All represent visible phenomena. Words alone were not sufficient to convince people of the trustworthiness of the Christian message. Along with the verbal message, God consistently confirmed the reliability of that message with works that could be explained only as above and beyond rational and natural happenings. In other words, God miraculously and supernaturally verified His message, both in the life of His Son and in the lives of those who first heard Him teach. For a time God even verified the reality of the Christian message in the lives of those who had never heard Christ personally.

The New Testament documents are filled with examples illustrating this dynamic process in the life of Christ, in the lives of the apostles, and in the lives of New Testament believers generally. In fact, the primary reason John wrote his Gospel was to verify the deity and message of Christ by referring to the miracles He performed. This is why he culminated this Gospel with the following summation: "Jesus did many other *miraculous signs* in the presence of His disciples, which are not recorded in this book. But these [miraculous signs] are written that you may believe that Jesus is the Christ, the Son of God, and that by believing you may have life in his name" (John 20:30-31).

The Book of Acts records this process as it continued in the lives of the apostles and in multitudes of New Testament believers who responded to their message. Following the miracles of Pentecost, involving the mighty rushing wind that filled the house where they were waiting in Jerusalem as Jesus had commanded and the tongues of fire that fell upon them, Peter stood up to preach. Significantly, He bridged the gap between their present experience with supernatural phenomena (wind, fire, and tongues) and the miracles that accompanied Christ's message when He was on earth. "Men of Israel," he proclaimed, "listen to this: Jesus of Nazareth was a man *accredited* by God to you by *miracles, wonders* and *signs,* which God did among you through him, as you yourselves know" (Acts 2:22).

Following Peter's invitation to believe in Christ, about three thousand were baptized. And then we read that these new Christians "devoted themselves to the apostles' *teaching*. . . . Everyone was filled with awe, and many *wonders* and *miracles* were done by the apostles" (Acts 2:42,43). Consequently, many more people believed in Christ and "were added to their number daily" (Acts 2:47).

The picture is clear. First, Christ's deity and message were verified by supernatural happenings. Then the church was launched in the same way. And as the apostles continued to teach the message of Christ, that very message was verified with many more wonders and miracles. There was no way to deny its *trustworthy* nature.

Intricately related to this miraculous process by which God confirmed the message of Christianity was God's bestowal of spiritual gifts on New Testament believers. This is why the Hebrew author stated that "God also testified to it by signs, wonders and various miracles, and *gifts of the Holy Spirit*" (Heb. 2:4). In fact, the gift of teaching, which was no doubt given to the apostles primarily, was just as miraculous as the miracles that accompanied the use of that gift. It appears that this was one of the primary gifts that enabled the apostles to become channels through which the "trustworthy message" came. It was no doubt this spiritual gift that Jesus was referring to when He said to these men, "The Counselor, the Holy Spirit, whom the Father will send in my name, will *teach you* all things and will remind you of everything I have said to you" (John 14:26). And later Jesus also said, "I have much more to say to you, more than you can now bear. But when he, the Spirit of truth, comes, he will *guide you into all truth*" (John 16:12,13). In other words, Jesus had conveyed many things to the apostles that they could not recall on their own. In addition, the Lord had many more things to say that they were not yet ready to comprehend. Eventually, after the Lord had returned to heaven, the Holy Spirit came upon them and first reminded them of what Christ had already taught them and then taught them additional truth. This process was a dramatic fulfillment of Christ's promise, and was carried forward when these New Testament believers in Jerusalem continued in the "apostles' *teaching*" (Acts 2:42). At this point these men were speaking the message of Christ by direct revelation—a miracle in itself. Furthermore, this miraculous process was accompanied by additional miracles to add validity to their message.

There were many more spiritual gifts bestowed on the New

Testament believers as a result of the apostles' initial ministry. The Corinthians illustrate this phenomenon more than any other group of New Testament Christians. More important, however, to this discussion is the fact that these gifts were a means not only to confirm the message of Christ, but also to confirm the reality of that message in the Corinthians' lives. Thus Paul begins his letter by saying, "I always thank God for you because of his *grace* given you in Christ Jesus. For in him you have been enriched in every way—in all your *speaking* and in all your *knowledge*—because our testimony about Christ was *confirmed* in you. Therefore, you do not lack any *spiritual gift* as you eagerly wait for our Lord Jesus Christ to be revealed" (1 Cor. 1:4-8). Obviously, it was the spiritual gifts that came upon the Corinthians that miraculously verified the reality of their spiritual experience.

In conclusion, Paul instructed Titus to appoint as elders men who held firmly to the "trustworthy message" as it had been faithfully taught, first by Christ and then by those who heard Him. And to those who were exposed to the miraculous process that accompanied the revelation of this message, there was no question that it was indeed *trustworthy*. God did not leave it to chance. He wanted the whole world to know that He had indeed spoken.

B. The Message—The Overseer's Response in Attitudes and Actions

Though we have spent considerable time giving "behind-the-scenes" information to explain *why* the message Paul was referring to was trustworthy, the primary burden of the apostle's instruction to Titus was the way the spiritual leaders were to view the message and how they were to use it in the lives of others.

1. *Hold firmly to it*

A man who was appointed to be an elder in Crete "must *hold firmly* to the trustworthy message." He was not to waver in his convictions regarding its reliability. Nor was he to deviate from its total message. As Paul wrote to Timothy, every elder was to do his best to present himself to God as one approved, "a workman who does not need to be ashamed and who *correctly handles the word of truth*" (2 Tim. 2:15).

2. *Encourage others with it*

An elder who "held firmly to the trustworthy message" would be able to "encourage others by sound doctrine." In fact, this was a primary purpose of Scripture. Those who were teaching false doctrine in Crete were discouraging people and were leading them astray to such an extent that Paul wrote, "They are ruining whole households by teaching things they ought not to teach" (Titus 1:11).

The Thessalonians represent another church where incomplete doctrine and/or false doctrine discouraged and confused people. For example, some did not understand what happened to believers who died before the second coming of Christ. Paul explained that "the dead in Christ will rise first. After that, we who are still alive and are left will be caught up with them in the clouds to meet the Lord in the air. And so we will be with the Lord forever. Therefore," Paul wrote, "*encourage each other with these words*" (1 Thess. 4:16-18).

Some of these believers in Thessalonica were also confused regarding the coming judgment on this earth. Some believed that Christians would be subject to God's judgments during this period of tribulation. Not so, wrote Paul. "For God did not appoint us to suffer wrath but to receive salvation through our Lord Jesus Christ. He died for us so that, whether we are awake or asleep, we may live together with him. Therefore, *encourage one another* and build each other up just as in fact you are doing" (1 Thess. 5:9-11). Once again we see the use of sound doctrine to encourage believers.

3. *Refute those who oppose it*

In every situation there will be people who distort God's truth. This was Paul's concern when he met with the Ephesian elders in Meletus. "Guard yourselves and all the flock of which the Holy Spirit has made you overseers," he said. "Be shepherds of the church of God, which he bought with his own blood. I know that after I leave, savage wolves will come in among you and will not spare the flock. Even from your own number men will arise and *distort the truth* in order to draw away disciples after them. So be on your guard!" (Acts. 20:28-31).

It is an elder's responsibility to refute those who are in opposition to sound doctrine. And in Crete, as in Ephesus, Paul's primary concern was to protect Christians from false teachers who were attempting to lead people astray for selfish reasons. It goes without saying, of course, that only those who know sound doctrine and who "hold firmly" to it can carry out this responsibility.

A TWENTIETH-CENTURY APPLICATION

From the vantage point of the twentieth century there are many people who raise questions regarding the message of Christianity. How do we know what Christ really taught? After all, nearly two thousand years have passed since He walked the earth. How can we really be sure the Bible is trustworthy and reliable?

These are valid questions. Fortunately, for the person who is sincerely searching for truth, there are very satisfactory answers. In fact, there is far more evidence that the biblical documents are reliable and trustworthy than there is to demonstrate the same conclusions for most other historical documents many people accept without question. For example, consider this statement by New Testament scholar Harold J. Greenlee:

> The oldest known manuscripts of most of the Greek classical authors are dated a thousand years or more after the author's death. The time interval for the Latin authors is somewhat less, varying down to a minimum of three centuries in the case of Virgil. In the case of the New Testament, however, two of the most important manuscripts were written within three hundred years after the New Testament was completed, and some virtually complete New Testament books as well as extensive fragmentary manuscripts of the New Testament date back to one century from the original writings.[3]

There are many specific secular documents that could be used to illustrate what Greenlee is referring to, not only in relationship to time lapse between original manuscripts and extant copies but also regarding the number of such copies. For example consider Caesar's *Gallic War*, which was composed between 58 and 50 B.C. Of the extant manuscripts in existence, only ten are good, and the oldest was written approximately nine hundred years later than Caesar's day. Few people, of course, doubt the reliability of these manuscripts to reconstruct this historical happening.

By contrast, we have at our disposal approximately five thousand Greek manuscripts that contain all or part of the New Testament. And in addition, most of the New Testament can be reproduced from quotations made by the early church fathers who wrote during the second and third centuries. In fact, one scholar found the entire New Testament in the works of the early church fathers with the exception of eleven verses.

To doubt the reliability of the New Testament in giving us a correct record of what Christ and His followers taught is to deny reality. As John Warwick Montgomery wrote, "To be skeptical of the resultant text of the New Testament books is to allow all of classical antiquity to slip into obscurity for no documents of the ancient period are as well attested bibliographically as the New Testament."[4]

We do have a "trustworthy message." In fact, we have far more information at our disposal than Titus did. In addition, many of the letters written to New Testament churches repeat basic Christian doctrines, demonstrating the consistency of the Bible. For example, the letter to the Ephesians contains almost every important doctrine of Christianity. The same is true of the Thessalonian letters and the Roman letter. Each of these Epistles contains sufficient truth to build a basic system of theology for the New Testament church.

More important to most of us, however, is not what we believe about the Bible (most of us believe it is a trustworthy document), but what we do with the Bible. Are we holding firmly to it? Are we using it to encourage others? Do we even know it well enough to refute those who oppose it?

Perhaps this last question is the key. How well do *you*

know the Bible? We cannot use it if we do not know it. And we cannot know it if we do not read and study it.

Obviously, spiritual leaders in the church have a greater responsibility to study and learn the Bible so they can teach it to others. This was Paul's concern in appointing elders in Crete. A qualified elder had to hold firmly to the trustworthy message as it had been taught so that he could "encourage others by sound doctrine and refute those who oppose[d] it." But today all believers have at their disposal the trustworthy message. We can read it, study it, and apply it to our own lives. But we can also read it and study in order to be functioning members of Christ's body. As Paul stated to the Thessalonians, we are to "encourage one another and build each other up" (1 Thess. 5:11). And to the Romans Paul said, "I myself also am convinced that you yourselves are full of goodness, *filled with all knowledge,* and able also to admonish one another" (Rom. 15:14, NASB). Obviously, the basis for encouraging and admonishing other believers is a knowledge of the Bible, the eternal Word of God.

A PERSONAL LIFE RESPONSE

1. How often do you personally read the Bible?
2. How often do you seriously study the Bible (either in a group or as an individual)?
3. Can you use the Bible to show someone how to be saved?
4. Can you use the Bible to show someone how to be sure of his or her salvation?
5. Can you use the Bible to prove the deity of Christ—that Christ was God in the flesh?
6. Can you use the Bible to prove the Trinity—that God is one, yet three persons: Father, Son, and Holy Spirit?
7. Can you use the Bible to show someone that Chist is coming again?

NOTES

[1]Bible scholars are not sure who wrote the Epistle to the Hebrews. Many believe it was Paul. Others think it may have been Apollos or some other person mentioned in the New Testament. There is really no way to be completely sure. There is, however, abundant evidence that it is indeed a reliable New Testament document inspired by the Holy Spirit.

[2]C. S. Lewis, *Mere Christianity* (New York: Macmillian, 1952), pp. 40, 41.

[3]Harold J. Greenlee, *Introduction to New Testament Textual Criticism* (Grand Rapids: Eerdmans, 1964), p. 16.

[4]John Warwick Montgomery, *History and Christianity* (Downers Grove, Ill.: InterVarsity, 1971), p. 20.

Chapter VI

False Teachers—How to Handle Them

SOMETHING TO THINK ABOUT

How would you describe people you have met who were involved in believing and teaching false doctrine?

- ☐ They are sincere but ignorant.
- ☐ They are trying to earn their way to heaven.
- ☐ Their motives are completely false.
- ☐ They are "in it" for the money.
- ☐ They are purposely deceiving others.

A LOOK AT PAUL'S LETTER

The Problem in Crete—False Teachers

1:10 For there are many rebellious people, — a
mere talkers — b } 1
and deceivers, — c
especially those of the circumcision group.

1:11 They must be silenced,
2 { a —because they are ruining whole households
b —by teaching things they ought not to teach—
c —and that for the sake of dishonest gain.

1:12 Even one of their own prophets has said,
"Cretans are always liars, — a
evil brutes, — b } 3
lazy gluttons." — c

Paul's Proposed Solution

1:13 This testimony is true.
Therefore, rebuke them sharply,
so that they will be sound in faith and
will pay no attention to
Jewish myths or
to the commands of those who reject the truth.

Paul's Added Explanation

1:15 To the pure, all things are pure,
but to those who are corrupted
and do not believe,
nothing is pure.
In fact, both their minds and consciences
are corrupted. } 1

1:16 They claim to know God,
but by their actions
they deny Him.
They are detestable,
disobedient
and unfit for doing anything good. } 2

WHAT DID PAUL SAY?

A. The Problem in Crete—False Teachers

1. Their characteristics
   a. Rebellious
   b. Being mere talkers
   c. Deceiving
2. Their works
   a. Ruining whole households
   b. Teaching false doctrine
   c. Seeking dishonest gain
3. Reports of an inside witness
   a. They are liars
   b. They are evil brutes
   c. They are lazy gluttons

B. Paul's Proposed Solution

1. The method—rebuke

2. The purpose—restoration and protection

C. Paul's Added Explanation

1. They have defiled minds and consciences

2. They are even using the name of God for their own ends

WHAT DID PAUL MEAN?

Paul had several specific purposes in mind when he left Titus in Crete, but one stands out boldly in the first chapter. Generally, he was to "straighten out what was left unfinished" and to "appoint elders in every town" (1:5). But specifically, part of this overall process involved confronting false teachers in Crete whose destructive influence had already become clearly evident. Let's look more specifically at the problem.

A. The Problem in Crete—False Teachers

Paul clearly outlined the problem beginning with verse 10. First, he listed the specific traits and characteristics of false teachers. Then he specified the nature of their works and, finally, he supported his observations with a quotation from one of their philosophers or "prophets."

1. *Their characteristics*

"For there are *many* rebellious people, mere talkers and deceivers and especially those of the circumcision group," wrote Paul (1:10). The extent of this problem is immediately obvious. There were "many" of these individuals. Already they had permeated the church. Something had to be done to counteract their negative influence, which had reached very destructive proportions.

Paul first of all classified them as "rebellious" or "unruly." If they were ever subtle and secret, they were so no more. They were obviously in direct opposition to true Christian principles. And they were out to undermine all of the previous work that Paul and Titus had done in the area of evangelism and edification.

Paul also called them "mere talkers," that is, individuals who talked a lot, but whose words had very little substance. Though they were communicating constantly, they were saying nothing significant compared with the "trustworthy message" revealed by Jesus Christ and the Holy Spirit. Unfortunately, and ironically, false teachers do not have to say anything really substantive to lead people astray.

Thirdly, Paul identified these people as "deceivers."

Their motives were false and deceitful. Though they could certainly be classified as "self-deceived," they were well aware of what they were doing. They had clear-cut goals and premeditated strategies. This Paul made very clear in the next verse.

But before we move on to their specific "works," note that Paul gives us a clue in verse 10 as to the nature of their doctrine. Though these individuals no doubt represented a variety of viewpoints, a rather large segment was classified by Paul as "the circumcision group." These men had evidently put together a message containing elements of Judaism and paganism—including both secular pagan thought and religious thought. This will become even more clear later in this passage.

2. *Their works*

Their *characteristics* were obvious, but closely interrelated with these traits are their *works*. They were "ruining *whole households* by teaching things they ought not to teach" (1:11).

One of the evangelistic strategies in the New Testament was to reach "whole households" with the gospel. This was a very productive approach. By reaching parents with the message of Christ, one can almost guarantee reaching everyone in the family.

This is dramatically illustrated when Paul's missionary team arrived in Philippi. Their first convert was Lydia and then "the members of her *household*" (Acts 16:15). Later they reached the Philippian jailer and "all his *family*" (Acts 16:33). When they arrived in Corinth, they won Crispus, the synagogue ruler, to Christ. Consequently "his entire *household* believed" (Acts 18:8).

The false teachers in Crete used the same strategy. Why not? A good method is a good method, no matter what the goal or the content of the message. Rather than *reaching* whole households for Christ with the "trustworthy message" of Christianity, they were "*ruining* whole households" with false doctrine.

Furthermore, their motives were all wrong. This is why

Paul called them "deceivers." Their primary concern was not the spiritual welfare of these people, but rather their own material interests. They were in the business of leading people astray for what they could get out of people for themselves—specifically, financial gain!

This explains why Paul insisted that a person appointed to eldership was to be a man who was "not pursuing dishonest gain" (1:7). Of all Paul's concerns, this was predominant in his thinking and teaching. It represents one of the most conscientious concerns in his own ministry. Often he would not even receive what he was entitled to so that he might keep his own motives clear in the eyes of those he was ministering to, especially non-Christians (1 Cor. 9:1-18; 1 Thess. 2:9).

Don't misunderstand. Paul is not opposed to financial remuneration for spiritual leaders. In fact, he insisted that "elders who direct the affairs of the church well are worthy of double honor"; that is, material support (1 Tim. 5:17). But this was not to be their motive. Their primary concern was to be the spiritual welfare of people.

By contrast, the false teachers in Crete were motivated by one basic thing—their own selfish interests. They were completely unconcerned about what happened to people spiritually.

3. *An inside witness*

Paul was an amazingly outspoken person. But what he said he wanted to be sure of. To support his accusations and conclusions, he quoted one of the Cretan philosophers, probably Epiminides, who lived about six hundred years before Christ. "Even one of their prophets has said," quoted Paul, that "Cretans are always liars, evil brutes, lazy gluttons" (1:12).

The correlations are obvious. "Liars" are "deceivers." "Evil brutes" are animals who prey on innocent victims, tearing them to shreds. And "lazy gluttons" have in mind their own selfish interests and needs and couldn't care less how they achieve these goals. Such were the false teachers in Crete. They were like "savage wolves" who were destroying the flock of God (Acts 20:29).

Obviously, Paul had met this kind of person before. He of course was not condemning all Cretans by this quotation. Rather, he was simply pointing out that what a non-Christian Cretan observed regarding the Cretans' philosophy of life was actually being demonstrated by false teachers who were at work among the Christians in Crete.

B. Paul's Proposed Solution

The apostle Paul not only had the ability to come directly to the point when dealing with problems in the New Testament church, but he also offered solutions. Some people today are expert at analyzing difficulties but offer few suggestions for eliminating the difficulties. Not so with Paul.

Epiminides' "testimony is true" wrote Paul. And with this acknowledgment, the apostle was demonstrating another New Testament principle he was committed to. We must face the reality of problems. Surely, unless the church in Crete did so, it was doomed to destruction. And just as Paul "faced the reality of problems," he also faced what was necessary to *solve* those problems. Already he had written that "they must be silenced" (1:11), but now he succinctly spells out *how:* "Rebuke them sharply" (1:13).

Note at this juncture that Paul is not laying this burden on Titus alone. Already he has carefully outlined a much broader solution to the problem created by ungodly false teachers in Crete. This is the basic reason why Paul instructed Titus to "straighten out what was left unfinished and *appoint elders in every town.*" "Appointing elders" was not purely an organizational matter. Rather, it was a basic solution to the problems created by false teachers. Titus was to counteract their ungodly efforts and ungodly influence by strategically placing in leadership roles, first of all, men whose personal and family life style exemplified Jesus Christ and the truth concerning Him. Secondly, they were to be men who "must hold firmly to the trustworthy message as it has been taught." And for what purpose? So that they could "encourage others by sound doctrine and *refute those who oppose*[*d*] *it*" (1:9).

"Rebuke them sharply" is an exhortation, then, to *all* the elders in the Cretan church. There was no way for one man to resolve this problem. Already the influence of these people was widespread. Already "whole households" were crumbling. It would take a multiple force of godly leaders permeating the body of Christ to turn the tide.

But notice also another of Paul's basic concerns. Though he had made some very strong statements about these false leaders, he still had their own spiritual welfare at heart. He still had hope that they would acknowledge the truth. Thus, a basic purpose for this kind of rebuke was not only to restore and protect other Cretans who had been negatively influenced by them, but to restore and protect these individuals themselves. Paul made this clear when he wrote, "Therefore, rebuke them sharply, so that they will be sound in the faith [*restored* doctrinally] and will pay no attention to Jewish myths or to the commands of those who reject the truth [*protected* doctrinally]" (1:13,14).

Here again Paul gives us another clue as to the nature of the false teachings that were being disseminated in Crete. Earlier he had referred to "the circumcision group" (1:10); here he referred to "Jewish myths" and the "commands of men."

No doubt Titus was facing in Crete some of the same problems Timothy was facing in Ephesus. This is why Paul wrote to Timothy in his first letter:

> As I urged you when I went into Macedonia, stay there in Ephesus so that you may command certain men not to teach *false doctrines* any longer nor to devote themselves to *myths and endless genealogies*. These promote controversies rather than God's work—which is by faith. The goal of this command is love, which comes from a pure heart, a good conscience and a sincere faith. Some have wondered away from these and turned to *meaningless talk*. They want to be teachers of the law, but they do not know what they are talking about or what they so confidently affirm (1 Tim. 1:3-7).

As we will see however, the nature of the problem in Ephesus was probably somewhat different. The men in Crete had apparently fallen to a far greater depth than had those in Ephesus. This is why Paul's solution in both situations is quite different. And this is why he needed to elaborate on what he had just said to Titus.

C. Paul's Added Explanation

Paul evidently felt it was necessary to elaborate on the problem in Crete as well as on his proposed solution. Legitimately, and especially from our twentieth-century perspective, we could ask the question "Why such a severe approach?" And the question is even more logical when you consider other statements Paul made about how to handle those who are in error theologically. For example, consider his words to Timothy in his second letter:

> Don't have anything to do with foolish and stupid arguments, because you know they produce quarrels. And the Lord's servant must not quarrel; instead, he must be *kind* to everyone, able to teach, not resentful. Those who oppose him he must *gently instruct,* in the hope that God will give them a change of heart leading them to a knowledge of the truth, and that they will come to their senses and escape from the trap of the devil, who has taken them captive to do his will" (2 Tim. 2:23-26).

Or consider also Paul's exhortation to the Galatians: "Brothers, if a man is trapped in some sin, you who are spiritual should *restore him gently*. But watch yourself; you also may be tempted" (Gal. 6:1).

In Paul's letter to Titus there is a decided difference in his approach. There is little reference to the "gentleness" we sense in these previous exhortations.

Is this a contradiction—a change in his philosophy of discipline? Not at all. The reason for Paul's approach to the problems in Crete becomes very clear when you study more carefully the nature of the problems and the characteristics of these men who were creating them. The difficulties in Crete were beyond the stage of "gentle dialogue." Titus was facing people who were totally corrupt, people who had consciously rejected the "trustworthy message." They had deliberately chosen the path of corruption and unbelief. To them nothing was pure. "In fact," Paul wrote, "both their minds [the way they think] and consciences [the way they feel] are corrupted" (1:15). When this combination is true of a person, he has reached the lowest point in degeneration. He is no longer self-deceived but deliberately setting out to thwart God's purpose.

And what made this problem even worse, they had purposely mixed truth with error in order to deceive more people. Thus Paul wrote, "They claim *to know God,* but by their actions they deny Him" (1:16). How could any person lower himself to the place where he used the name of God for purely selfish purposes? This these men did! And when this happened, Paul showed little mercy. This explains why he used certain words to describe them. "They are *detestable, disobedient* and *unfit for doing anything good*" (1:16). In other words, a "gentle approach" could only serve to further their own selfish endeavors. There's only one way to reach men who deliberately lie, who destroy people's families without a twinge of conscience, and who rip people off "in the name of God." They must be directly confronted with the Word of God by godly persons whose motives are pure and whose life styles exemplify the characteristics of Jesus Christ. Paul's hope was that these men would respond to this approach. And, even more so, he wanted the body of Christ in Crete delivered from their destructive influence.

A TWENTIETH-CENTURY APPLICATION

Developing a Proper Cultural Perspective

Though there are many false teachers in today's world who are disseminating doctrines that contradict the Word of God, there are probably few that have reached the state of deterioration those in Crete had reached. In fact, few had reached that state even in the New Testament. Paul was definitely dealing with an *extreme* situation calling for an *extreme* solution.

Furthermore, what happened specifically in Crete seldom happens in our western culture, which has been permeated with the Hebrew-Christian ethic and philosophy of life. Why is this true? To answer this question we must reconstruct the first-century cultural dynamics in Crete. First, Paul and Titus had penetrated a totally pagan culture with the gospel of Christ. Most converts were "true" Cretans; that is, individuals given over to a selfish and sensuous life style devoid of any Hebrew or Christian influence. Their religion was predominantly pagan, with the exception of those who had imbibed some perverted concepts from Judaism and syncretized these ideas with their own. Apparently it was these individuals who were most active as false teachers attempting to compete with Paul and Titus.

To complicate matters, it also appears that these individuals professed to be "Christians" and became an integral part of the church. Consequently, they had an inside track for achieving their insidious goals. This tactic should not surprise us, since selfish and sensual people will do anything to achieve their own ends. After all, they had syncretized paganism and Judaism. Why not add a third religion—Christianity. If it would enable them to make a "fast buck," why not?

And of course people who respond to a new religious message are very open and vulnerable to being taught anything that sounds acceptable. The false teachers understood these dynamics, and before Paul and Titus could ground the new Christians and develop mature leaders to guide them, they arose from within and began to take over. "We'll guide you and teach you," they said. And thus we discover a very destructive influence that quickly reached advanced states—even "ruining whole households."

The only way to resolve this problem was to launch a Christian counterattack. This Paul did by leaving Titus in Crete to appoint mature Christian leaders who would permeate the churches with sound doctrine, refuting those who were leading people astray. "They must be silenced" wrote Paul (1:11), and the only way to do it was to "encourage others with sound doctrine and refute those who oppose it" (1:9). With this approach Paul even hoped to see some of these false teachers truly converted to Christ.

Some Twentieth-Century Lessons

Though these exact events are somewhat far removed from most twentieth-century church situations, there are some dynamic lessons that emerge for twentieth-century Christians.

1. It is important, especially in starting churches, to ground new believers in sound doctrine. If we don't, there are many false teachers abroad who can very quickly infiltrate and lead people astray.
2. It is important to appoint mature Christian leaders as soon as possible to shepherd these new churches. If we don't, immature leaders will naturally arise and create problems.
3. Spiritual leaders must be selected and appointed according to the qualifications outlined for elders and specified in the New Testament in 1 Timothy 3 and Titus 1. Immature leaders in the church will do more harm than good.
4. The norm in the New Testament for local churches is multiple leadership. It takes a multiple force of godly men to keep a church growing and maturing spiritually. The more Christlike personal and family models there are in a given local church, the stronger the influence for Christ and the easier to keep false teachers and false practices from arising.
5. False teachers and false doctrine must be dealt with immediately. However, it must be done according to biblical principles and guidelines:

   First, it is a task for the elders of the church. They must not ignore the problem.

   Second, we must make sure it is indeed false doctrine. People have sometimes been falsely accused because not all the facts were in. Never accept accusations second hand. And if an elder is involved, Paul states that we are not to "entertain an accusation against an elder unless it is brought by two or three witnesses" (1 Tim. 5:9).

Third, we must make sure the person is approached properly. Paul's instructions are that in the beginning stages we must take a very sensitive and gentle approach with the hope that we can "restore" them, leading them to a knowledge of the truth" (Gal. 6:1; 2 Tim. 2:24-26).

Fourth, we must always give the person a second chance. Paul even specified this approach for the false teachers in Crete as he culminated his letter: "But avoid foolish controversies and genealogies and arguments and quarrels about the law, because these are unprofitable and useless. Warn a divisive person once, and then warn him a second time. After that, have nothing to do with him. You may be sure that such a man is warped and sinful; he is self-condemned" (Titus 3:9-11).

A PERSONAL LIFE RESPONSE

Meditate on the following Scriptures and evaluate your own attitudes and actions in relationship to the body of Christ:

"Live in harmony with one another" (Rom. 12:16).

"Make every effort to do what leads to peace" (Rom. 14:19).

"Watch out for those who cause divisions" (Rom. 16:17).

"Be of one mind, live in peace" (2 Cor. 13:11).

"Make every effort to keep the unity of the Spirit through the bond of peace" (Eph. 4:3).

"Make my joy complete by being like-minded, having the same love, being one in spirit and purpose" (Phil. 2:2).

Chapter VII

A Profile for Men

SOMETHING TO THINK ABOUT

Is the knowledge of sound doctrine the primary means that causes people to live godly lives?

☐ YES

☐ NO

☐ UNCERTAIN

A LOOK AT PAUL'S LETTER

2:1 You must teach what is in accord with sound doctrine.

A Profile for Older Men

2:2

Teach the older men to be temperate, ——— 1
worthy of respect, ——— 2
self-controlled, ——— 3
and
sound in faith ——— 4
in love ——— 5
and
in endurance. . . . —— 6

A Profile for Young Men

2:6 Similarly, encourage the young men
to be self-controlled. — 1

2:7 In everything set them an example by doing what is good. ——— 2
In your teaching show integrity, ——— a
seriousness ——— b

2:8 and ——— c
soundness of speech that cannot be condemned, so that those who oppose you may be ashamed because they have nothing bad to say about us.

A Profile for Older Men

1. Temperate
2. Worthy of respect
3. Self-controlled
4. Sound in faith
5. Sound in love
6. Sound in endurance

A Profile for Young Men

1. Encourage self-control
2. Exemplify in your teaching:
   a. Integrity
   b. Seriousness
   c. Soundness of speech

WHAT DID PAUL MEAN?

Paul's theme throughout this dynamic letter to Titus is clearly "a profile for a Christian life style." By contrast, his primary concern was the ungodly life style of false teachers and, consequently, the way they were influencing the new Christians in Crete. This was foremost in Paul's mind when he charged Titus to remain in Crete to "straighten out what was left unfinished" (1:5).

These false teachers claim "to know God," wrote Paul, "but by their *actions* they deny Him. They are . . . unfit for doing *anything good*" (1:16).

Paul's master stroke for solving this problem was to appoint to eldership in Crete men who would combat their negative influence with a godly life style. Consequently, Paul very early in his letter enumerated those qualities that should characterize a spiritual leader's family life as well as those that should characterize his personal life.

In addition to moral and ethical guidance (concerning *how these men lived*), they were to be well-grounded in sound doctrine (concerning *what they believed*). And with this "trustworthy message" they were to encourage the new Christians and also to openly refute and rebuke false teachers who were leading them astray.

Paul's primary strategy for resolving this problem, however, was not teaching "sound doctrine" per se. If it had been, he would have spelled out carefully what this sound doctrine should be. Rather, he concentrated on what should *accompany* sound doctrine.

Paul's approach in this letter brings into focus a very serious methodological error that is prevalent in some Christian circles today. Some believe and teach that emphasizing "sound doctrine" will automatically result in a "godly life style." If this were true, Paul would not have spent the bulk of his letter spelling out what should *accompany* sound doctrine—what that life style should be, as it relates both to Christian leaders and to all members of Christ's body. And this leads us directly into the next paragraph in Paul's letter.

"You must teach," wrote Paul, "what is in accord with sound doctrine" (2:1).

Paul turned his attention from the leaders to all the members of Christ's body. Evidently, he felt it was necessary to become very *specific* regarding various segments of the church. Consequently, he instructed Titus as to what to say to older men, older women, young women, young men, and slaves. Furthermore, he specifically discussed behavioral expectations in their relationship to governing authorities, as well as their attitudes and actions toward the unsaved world at large. In this chapter, look at what Paul said should characterize Christian men in general—first those who are older and then those who are younger.

A. A Profile for Older Men

"Teach the older men," wrote Paul, "to be temperate, worthy of respect, self-controlled, and sound in faith, in love and in endurance" (2:2). Consider these qualities one by one.

1. *Temperate*

Paul gives a rather clear and enlarged perspective on what he means by this word in 1 Thessalonians 5—although here the translators of the New International Version use the word *self-controlled*. This can become a little confusing to the English reader, since the translators also render another word as "self-control" in the same list of qualities for older men. More about this later.

However, let's look more carefully at what Paul wrote to the Thessalonians. In chapter 5 he was speaking of the coming days of God's judgment on earth— days that he called the "day of the Lord" (5:2). Dealing specifically with this time period, Paul wrote:

> But you, brothers, are not in darkness so that this day should surprise you like a thief. You are all sons of the light and sons of the day. We do not belong to the night or to the darkness. So then, let us not be like others who are asleep, but let us be alert and *self-controlled* [that is, temperate or sober]. For those who sleep, sleep at night, and those who get

> drunk, get drunk at night. But since we belong to the day, let us be *self-controlled* [that is, temperate or sober], putting on faith and love as a breastplate, and the hope of salvation as a helmet (1 Thess. 5:4-8).

For a Christian to be "temperate" in the sense that Paul is using the word here is to be in control of his mental, emotional, and spiritual faculties. Surely, one who is under the influence of alcohol is not temperate or in control of himself. But obviously, Paul had more in mind than "drunkenness." A man who is reflecting a temperate life style has not lost his spiritual and psychological bearings. He has a proper Christian perspective on life and where history is heading. He is stable and steadfast, reflecting a clear mind, no matter what happens around him. As Thayer defined this word, a temperate person is characterized by a state untouched by any slumberous or beclouding influence.

2. *Worthy of respect*

This quality involves living in such a way that others respect us because of our Christian life style. We are *worthy* of respect, because we have earned it through imitating Christ's way of life. Many of the specifics of the spiritual qualities already outlined by Paul for elders in 1:7 combine to give a man this kind of reputation among both Christians and non-Christians. By not being overbearing, quick-tempered, given to wine, violent, and dishonest, a man will soon become worthy of respect. He will be honored and properly venerated for his Christian character.

3. *Self-controlled*

Here is a characteristic Paul referred to frequently in this little Epistle—five times, to be exact. We have already noted this characteristic as a quality for elders (1:8).

"Self-control" describes a more specific concept than "temperance" (which is sometimes used as a synonym for self-control). Temperance refers to an ability to have a proper perspective on life and history, a perspective that in turn affects our mental and emotional stability and reactions. Self-control zeros in more specifically on our fleshly appetites. As stated in an earlier chapter, a Christian—in this case, an older man—is not to be in bondage to fleshly desires, impulses, and passions.

4. *Sound in faith*

To be "sound"—a word used several times in Paul's letter to Titus—means to be "in good health." When used to describe "doctrine," it means to hold to true and incorrupt teachings. When used to describe faith and love and endurance, it refers to a healthy state in relationship to these spiritual qualities of life.

To be "sound in faith" focuses specifically on our attitudes toward God the Father and His Son, Jesus Christ. Faith, of course, is a synonym for trust and belief. To the extent that we have confidence in our Lord, we are spiritually healthy in the area of faith. If we are in a constant state of doubt and unbelief, we are certainly not "sound in faith."

The true test of faith is determined, to a large extent, by our actions. Faith, to be healthy, cannot be passive. It must be obvious in our lives—both by what we both say and what we do. That is why Paul could thank God for the Thessalonians' "work produced by faith" (1 Thess. 1:3). That is also why James wrote, "Faith by itself, if it is not accompanied by action, is dead. . . . Show me your faith without deeds, and I will show you my faith by what I do" (James 2:17,18).

5. *Sound in love*

Being sound in love is the hallmark of Christian maturity. Paul, when referring to faith, hope, and love, clearly stated that the greatest of these is love (1 Cor. 13:13).

Why is this so? Paul's definition of love in 1 Corinthians clearly answers this question:

> Love is patient, love is kind. It does not envy, it does not boast, it is not proud. It is not rude, it is not self-seeking, it is not easily angered, it keeps no record of wrongs. Love does not delight in evil but rejoices in the truth. It always protects, always trusts, always hopes, always preserves. Love never fails (1 Cor. 13:4-8).

To be "sound in love," then, means to live like Christ, for

it was these qualities of love that characterized *His* life. In the words of Paul to the Ephesians, we are to be "imitators of God, therefore, as dearly loved children and *live a life of love*, just as Christ loved us and gave himself up for us as a fragrant offering and sacrifice to God" (Eph. 5:1).

6. *Sound in endurance*

In the New Testament the concept of "endurance" (or "patience") is used to refer to a person who is unswerving in his commitment to Jesus Christ no matter what the problems and trials he faces. In this sense it is clearly aligned with "hope." In fact, Paul used the two words together in his letter to the Thessalonians when he thanked God for their "*endurance* inspired by *hope* in our Lord Jesus Christ" (1 Thess. 1:3).

A person who is "sound in endurance," then, is a Christian who is holding fast to what he believes, even though he finds himself in the midst of a multitude of difficulties. According to Paul, this is not a quality of life that is natural. Even a "man of God" must "pursue" this quality (1 Tim. 6:11).

These are the qualities that Paul was particularly concerned about in the lives of older men in the Cretan churches. Titus was to "teach" these men to become believers characterized by temperance, respect, and self-control and to be spiritually healthy in the areas of faith, love, and endurance.

B. A Profile for Young Men

Paul also instructed Titus to give some specific direction to young men regarding their life style. Note however, that Paul emphasized an added dimension in the communication process. After telling Titus to "encourage young men to be self-controlled"—the same quality discussed for older men in an earlier paragraph—he then exhorted Titus to "set them an example by *doing what is good*" (2:7).

Why this added emphasis? Obviously, Paul knew that these young men in Crete would be more critical of Titus because he was one of their peers. Consequently, he emphasized that Titus would have to take unusual precautions to make sure that *what* he taught was exemplified in his own life style.

Paul singles out three specific ways in which Titus should exemplify Jesus Christ in his teaching ministry: in integrity, in seriousness, and in soundness of speech. Let us look at each of these qualities individually.

1. *Integrity*

The word Paul used here literally means to be "uncorrupt." Though it is difficult to differentiate what Paul had in mind in this instance from what he refers to later as "soundness of speech," I personally believe he is exhorting Titus to make sure he "practices what he preaches"; that is, he was not to teach the young men one thing and live something else. If he did, he certainly would not win a hearing. And this leads to the next quality that was to characterize Titus's teaching ministry.

2. *Seriousness*

Here Paul is referring to that quality in a person's life that earns a right to be heard. Titus certainly could not expect young men his own age to respect him and take his words "seriously" unless they saw the same degree of "seriousness" in his life that he was asking of them. Again, Paul is emphasizing the importance of a Christian's total life style, particularly for those who are responsible as spiritual leaders.

3. *Soundness of speech*

This characteristic is yet another perspective on what should characterize Titus's teaching ministry. Paul is building a concept and he is using several words to explain what he had in mind. Titus was "to practice what he taught," i.e., show integrity in his teaching. He was "to earn a right to be heard" by winning respect. Also his content was to be carefully and accurately presented. Otherwise, those who were in opposition to Christ and the "trustworthy message" would be able to attack Titus justifiably and hurt the cause of Christ. On the contrary, if he "set them an example by doing what is good"—in everything and in every way—his opposition would be put to shame and ultimately silenced.

A TWENTIETH-CENTURY APPLICATION

Paul was writing specifically regarding the spiritual needs of men, both old and young, in a particular culture and at a particular time. But what he said emerges as a supracultural criterion for measuring our Christian life style and is applicable at any given moment in history.

But before we see how these qualities apply to twentieth-century Christian men, look at several lessons emerging from our study in Titus thus far that are more general in nature.

General Lessons

1. *Learning sound doctrine does not automatically result in a Christian life style.* If it did, Paul would have taken a much different approach in his letter to Titus. He would have emphasized selecting spiritual leaders primarily on the basis of what they believed (their theology), not by what characterized both their family and personal lives (their Christian life style). Obviously their doctrine *was* important, for they could not refute false teachers without an adequate knowledge of God's trustworthy message. But knowing the Bible without "living the Bible" simply produces more people who know the Bible but don't live it. And when this happens, the basic message of Christianity, though it may be accurate from a doctrinal point of view, soon becomes purely academic and is eventually nullified. In fact, it is my personal opinion that what Paul says in his letter to Titus is not an addendum to "sound doctrine"—it *is* sound doctrine—the doctrine of a Christian life style.
2. Second, and closely related to the first lesson, *people listen to people who not only know what they believe but are also living what they believe.* As we have noted, this is particularly true among peers. But it is also true of all age levels. Paul attacked the message of false teachers by appointing godly men who would counteract their negative influence. And he instructed Titus to be sure to exemplify in his own life what he was teaching and to be

sure to exemplify the message even by the *way* he taught it. This again points out why Paul throughout this letter emphasized "life style" rather than pure doctrine as a means of helping people mature spiritually. What people need today more than any other thing is to see and experience the Word of God "fleshed out" through the body of Christ as each member functions and as the body builds itself up in love (Eph. 4:16).

Specific Lessons for Older Men

1. *Regarding "temperance"*

Unfortunately, the older we get, the less guarantee we have that we will stabilize in our perspective on the Christian life. Our emotional state sometimes overshadows our spiritual state. In the twentieth-century world particularly, competition often threatens an older man more than it does a younger man. And in some instances, boredom also sets in because of too much leisure time. An older Christian needs to evaluate his life in the light of this mark of spiritual maturity.

A PERSONAL LIFE-RESPONSE QUESTION: Regarding your stability as a Christian, do you really have it together mentally, emotionally, and spiritually? If not, this should be an important goal for your life, seeking to do all you can with God's help to be this kind of person.

2. *Regarding being "worthy of respect"*

One of the most tragic problems among many members of Christ's body is a lack of mutual respect. How often have I heard, either directly or indirectly, "I really don't respect that person. He doesn't really live what he professes."

PERSONAL LIFE-RESPONSE QUESTIONS: What about your life? How much do people respect you? What have you done to win their respect? What goals do you need to establish and reach in order for this to happen?

3. *Regarding self-control*

The twentieth-century world, like the first-century world, caters to "the cravings of sinful man, lust of the eyes and his pride in possessions" (1 John 2:16). The apostle John wrote further: "Do not love the world or anything in the world. If anyone loves the world, the love of the Father is not in him" (1 John 2:15).

A PERSONAL LIFE-RESPONSE QUESTION: Are you living a self-controlled life in these areas outlined by John? Stop for a moment and think of specific things in your own life that you could list under each of the categories outlined by John 1) the cravings of sinful man, 2) the lust of the eyes, and 3) pride in possessions.

4. *Regarding being "sound in faith"*

A materialistic world—like the one we live in—militates against faith. In fact, it neutralizes the need for faith and the God we cannot see.

PERSONAL LIFE-RESPONSE QUESTIONS: To what extent do you really feel you need God? To what extent do you live by faith? If you were to remove every reference to faith in the Bible, would it really make much difference in the way you live?

5. *Regarding being "sound in love"*

Love is defined very selfishly and superficially in the twentieth-century world. In the Word of God, however, true love is defined by unselfish attitudes and actions towards others—not personal feelings.

PERSONAL LIFE-RESPONSE QUESTIONS: How do you measure up in patience? In kindness? Generosity? Humility? Courtesy? Unselfishness? Good temper? Guilelessness? Sincerity? These qualities are what the Bible defines as love.

6. *Regarding being "sound in endurance"*

The twentieth-century man wants what he wants when he wants it.

PERSONAL LIFE-RESPONSE QUESTIONS: How does "the impatient mentality" in our culture today affect your life spiritually? How willing are you to wait for God's timing in your life? Do you often take matters into your own hands, regardless of the situation?

A Specific Lesson for Young Pastors—or "Pastors-to-Be"

"DON'T LET ANYONE LOOK DOWN ON YOU BECAUSE YOU ARE YOUNG, BUT SET AN EXAMPLE FOR THE BELIEVERS IN SPEECH, IN LIFE, IN LOVE, IN FAITH AND IN PURITY" (1 Tim. 4:12).

Chapter VIII

A Profile for Women

SOMETHING TO THINK ABOUT

In his letter to Titus, Paul laid out a specific plan for teaching young women to live Christ-centered lives. Do you believe this strategy is cultural or supracultural? Why or why not?

A LOOK AT PAUL'S LETTER

A Profile for Older Women

2:3 Likewise
teach the older women
to be reverent in the way they live, —— 1
not to be slanderers —— 2
or
addicted to much wine, —— 3
but
to teach what is good. —— 4

A Profile for Younger Women

2:4 Then they can
train the younger women
to love their husbands —— 1
and
children, —— 2
2:5 to be self-controlled —— 3
and
pure, —— 4
to be busy at home, —— 5
to be kind, —— 6
and
to be subject to their husbands, —— 7
so that no one will malign the word of God.

WHAT DID PAUL SAY?

A Profile for Older Women

1. "Reverent" in life style
2. Not given to slander
3. Not addicted to wine
4. Teaching what is good

A Profile for Younger Women

1. Loving to their husbands
2. Loving to their children
3. Self-controlled
4. Pure
5. Busy at home
6. Kind
7. Submissive

WHAT DID PAUL MEAN?

Up to this point in his letter to Titus Paul has directed his thoughts primarily to men. Though what he has written certainly does not exclude women in terms of what should or should not characterize a Christian life style, he now clearly turns his attention *specifically* to women.

A. A Profile for Older Women

As with men, Paul was first of all concerned with those women who were older, not just spiritually, but chronologically. The reason, as we will see, was that Paul wanted them to be godly examples to the younger women.

1. *"Reverent" in life style*

Paul was concerned that the women who claimed to follow Christ should exemplify His life style. To "be reverent in the way they live" actually means that they were to live a life consistent with the fact that they claimed to be followers of God.

Again it is clear that Paul is drawing a contrast between the false teachers in Crete and those who are true Christians. Previously he had described these people as those who "claim to know God, but by their actions . . . deny Him" (1:16). In other words, they were *not* living lives that were consistent with the nature of God and Christ.

Paul's concern, then, was that Titus teach these Cretan Christians what is "in accord with sound doctrine"—that there might be no contradiction between their basic theological beliefs about God and Christ and the way they were living. This is in essence what he meant when he wrote that older women were to "be reverent in the way they live."

This kind of consistent life style was, of course, to characterize *all* Christians, whether men or women. This is why Paul begins this paragraph directed to women with the transitional word *likewise*, which refers back to what he has just said to older men. It is as if he is going to say the same thing to "older women" that he has just said to "older men." In essence this is what he does, but with a special emphasis just for women.

2. *Not given to slander*

How to use the tongue appropriately is a recurring problem for all human beings. And though it is certainly an area of weakness for both men and women, Paul specifically zeros in on this problem for women.

James dealt with this problem rather extensively in his letter to New Testament believers, pointing out graphically that a Christian's tongue serves as a precise measurement of Christian maturity (James 3:2). If we can control our tongue, he stated, we can usually control every other part of our personality.

To get his point across, James used three descriptive illustrations. With a *tiny* bit we can control a *large* horse; with a *small* rudder (relatively speaking) we can direct the course of a *huge* ship; and with a *little* spark we can set a *great* forest on fire (James 3:3-6). James then made the application: the "tongue is a *small* part of the body, but it makes *great* boasts. . . . It corrupts the *whole* person" (James 3:5-6).

The most serious consequence of a tongue "out of control" is what it does to other people. This is what Paul had in mind when he exhorted Titus to teach older women not to slander others. Malicious gossip is horribly destructive. It creates the opposite result of what Christians are to do for one another—it tears others down rather than builds them up. On the one hand, words can be "like a club or a sword or a sharp arrow" when used to hurt people (Prov. 25:18). On the other hand, words spoken at the right time and in the right way are "like apples of gold in settings of silver" (Prov. 25:11).

3. *Not addicted to wine*

Persistent drinking and drunkenness were common problems in the first-century world—as they have been throughout history. Many people converted to Christ had developed this kind of life style, women included. In fact, many women no doubt used wine as a means of coping with anxiety and stress caused by the way they were treated by men. It was a rather common practice for a man to consider his wife a slave, a convenience, a bearer of children in order to enhance his reputation in the community.

Coming to know Christ changed women's status. Paul wrote that in Christ there is neither "male nor female." We "are all one" (Gal. 3:28). In Christ we are heirs together "of the gracious gift of life" (1 Peter 3:7). But having a new spiritual position does not automatically change a person's self-image or immediately break old habits. Usually this is a process.

Evidently some of the older women in Crete, even as Christians, were still drinking too much. The word *addicted* as used by Paul in this letter to Titus, actually means being "in bondage" or being a "slave" to wine. This, Paul wrote, is not a mark of maturity, nor should it be a part of a Christian's life style. Thus Paul instructed Titus to teach the older women who were having this difficulty *not* to be "addicted to much wine." As people who were now Christians and new creatures in Christ, they were to break away from their old hurtful habits.

4. *Teaching what is good*

In describing the qualities that should characterize the life style of an older Christian woman, Paul zeroed in on two overarching positive qualities. First, they were to be "reverent in the way they live" and second, they were to "teach what is good." Again we see a classic pattern in Paul's approach to Christian communication, a pattern that is obvious throughout his letter to Titus. An overall godly life style was to form the basis for effective verbal teaching. The life lived in *accordance* with sound doctrine would enable these women to effectively communicate with younger women how to walk in the will of God, which Paul classified as *good* and pleasing and perfect (Rom. 12:2). Thus Paul introduced verse 4 by saying, "Then they can train the younger women"—that is, if they are living as they should, they will be able to communicate effectively. And this leads us to the next section in this chapter.

B. A Profile for Younger Women

Before we look at the individual qualities specified by Paul for younger women, note that he did not instruct Titus to take primary responsibility for teaching the younger women. This was a job for the older women.

There are probably several reasons for this approach. First, Titus was a young man himself—and probably single. There are always inherent dangers involved when young single men teach younger women, particularly married women, and especially in a culture like that of Crete. Second, what these young women needed to learn could best be learned through the modeling process—by observing older women with whom they could identify. Third, and perhaps most important, this was the most logical and sensible way to get the job done. Already Paul had instructed Titus to select elders who would carry the primary responsibility of modeling Christ and teaching others. And it follows that the most efficient way to multiply his ministry among women was to teach older women who in turn could train the younger. It represents an excellent plan for discipling others.

1. *Loving to their husbands*

One of the first things young married women were to learn was to "love their husbands." Why was this necessary? First, many of these women may have been married to men they really were not attracted to. In some cultures marriages are arranged by parents, regardless of romantic feelings. This was probably true also in Crete.

Second, many women in the first century, as already stated, were used as marital conveniences to produce offspring. There is usually no real sense of commitment, security, or fondness under these circumstances.

This brings us to a very important observation. The common word meaning "to love" in the New Testament is *agapao*. It refers to a *love* that does the right thing no matter what one's feelings are. It was this kind of love that sent Jesus Christ to the cross, even though, in His humanity, He prayed in the garden that He might be able to avoid the experience.

But He did the will of God because He knew this was the right thing to do—in spite of His feelings.

The Greek word used by Paul in Titus 2:4, however, is *phileo*—a word used to describe the "emotional" dimensions of human relationships. It involves friendship. It expresses delight and pleasure in doing something. This is why *agapao* is not used in the Bible specifically to describe "sexual love"—particularly sexual responsibility. "Sexual love" involves emotions and a person cannot be commanded to "feel" a certain way toward someone else. However, a person can be commanded to *do something* in spite of his feelings. For example, the Bible says, "Husbands *love* [in an *agape* sense] your wives," or, more dramatically, it says, "Love your enemies." But one cannot force a person to feel positive when he feels negative. Thus Paul worded the statement very carefully to Titus: older women were to "train the younger women to love their husbands."

This kind of love can be learned. And since the husband was now to love his wife as Christ loved the church—an unconditional *agapao* love—a wife would begin to discover a sense of security and emotional satisfaction that would make it possible for her to respond with warm feelings of attraction and commitment. One of the best ways to learn to respond this way would be to see it demonstrated in the lives of older women who modeled this kind of relationship with their own husbands.

2. *Loving to their children*

The phrase "to love their children" actually comes from one Greek word *(philoteknos),* which literally means to be "child-lovers." And again, as in our previous study on women learning to "love their husbands," Paul was referring to a phileo *love,* which definitely includes the emotional dimension in human relationships. These women in New Testament days were to learn to "love their children," that is, to have positive feelings toward their offspring.

Their difficulty in loving their children probably relates to the same reasons for their difficulty in loving their husbands. Bearing children as a result of "dutiful performance" doesn't set a very good stage for a love relationship between mother and children. Resentment toward a husband can be easily transferred to the children.

3. *Self-controlled*

Once again we encounter one of Paul's most repeated qualities of life in his letter to Titus. Like all Christians, young women were to be in control of their physical, psychological, and spiritual faculties. They were not to be in bondage to fleshly desires, impulses, and passions. This is a basic reason why Paul instructed young widows to remarry (1 Tim. 5:11-15).

4. *Pure*

Closely associated with the quality of "self-control" is purity. Marital fidelity in the Cretan culture was not a common practice. If a husband was getting his sexual satisfaction at a local house of prostitution, why should his wife be faithful to him?

The message of Christ that Paul and Titus preached to the people on the island of Crete cut straight across this kind of thinking. It was a new message—a message of purity, of loyalty in marriage, and of marital fidelity. In fact, Peter emphasized this quality of life for women who were married to unsaved husbands. It was to serve as a divine means to bring their husbands to salvation in Christ. Thus Peter wrote, "Wives, in the same way be submissive to your husbands so that, if any of them do not believe the word, they may be won over without talk by the behavior of their wives, when they see the *purity* and reverence of your lives" (1 Peter 3:1,2).

5. *Busy at home*

From a twentieth-century perspective, this may be one of the most controversial qualities stated in this list. However, most of the problems can be resolved by a proper interpretation of Scripture.

Paul had the same concern for young Ephesian widows who got "into the habit of being idle and going about from house to house. And," wrote Paul "not only do they become idlers, but also gossips and busybodies, saying things they ought not to." Consequently, Paul counseled these young women "to marry, to have children, to *manage their homes* and to give the enemy no opportunity for slander" (1 Tim. 5:13,14).

When Paul wrote that young women should be "busy at home," he was dealing with a woman's priorities. In the New Testament culture a woman found it difficult to function productively outside the context of family life. She had very little to do, other than get into difficulty—particularly moral difficulty. Consequently, Paul advised the young women to marry or, if they were married, to avoid being "busy" in places other than within their homes.

6. *Kind*

The basic Greek word *agathos,* translated "kind" in NIV, refers to excellence in any respect, by which someone or something may be said to be distinguished, or *good.* No doubt Dorcas stands out in Scripture as a unique illustration of the kind of woman Paul was describing. Her good deeds involved "helping the poor," and we are told exactly how she did this. The widows who had gathered to mourn her death held in their hands the "robes and other clothes" that Dorcas had made while she was still with them. She was a kind and generous woman who used her sewing skills to meet the needs of others (Acts. 9:36-43).

One of the most elaborate biblical commentaries, however, on what Paul had in mind when he instructed older women to teach younger women to be good or kind appears in his first letter to Timothy. Here he was dealing with the problem of widows who were old enough to be put on the church rolls for help. "No woman," wrote Paul, "may be put on the list of widows unless she is over sixty, has been faithful to her husband, and is well known for her *good* [kind] deeds." Then Paul explains what these good deeds were: "such as bringing up children, showing hospitality, washing the feet of the saints, helping those in trouble and devoting herself to all kinds of good deeds" (1 Tim. 5:9,10). Obviously, many of these "kind" expressions were culturally related to the needs of that day. However, they are illustrative of those things that reflect what Paul meant when he said that a mature Christian woman is "to be kind."

7. *Submission*

Many Christians (and non-Christians even more so) misinterpret what Paul and other writers of Scripture meant when they emphasized that wives were to be subject to their husbands. First, the Bible teaches that submission should be a mutual, reciprocal expression among all Christians. In other words, it is not a word used only for women (Eph. 5:21). Second, submission does not mean that wives should never express their opinions or feelings. To believe that it does is a severe violation of all of the "one another" concepts in the New Testament. Third, submission does not mean a wife should indulge in sin because her husband demands it. There are times when all Christians, including wives, must take seriously the requirement to "obey God rather than men" (Acts 5:29). And finally, submission certainly does not mean that a wife must subject herself to physical and psychological abuse that is beyond her ability to bear. The laws of both men and God protect a person from this kind of abuse.

Submission refers to an attitude of "teachableness" toward other members of the body of Christ. All of us are to be involved in this reciprocal relationship. However, the Bible also goes a step further and emphasizes submission on the part of wives toward their husbands. This is a consistent concept throughout the Bible. It even antedates the Fall. A woman was not to dominate or control her husband, but rather respect him as her God-ordained protector and leader.

This concept is still true within a Christian marriage. However, it must be pointed out that when a husband "loves his wife as Christ loved the church," submission becomes a very natural and easy thing for wives to do. In fact, if both partners are committed to Jesus Christ, it is possible for a Christian couple actually to experience on a day-to-day basis the benefits of equality. In other words, a husband will not have to operate as "the boss." In fact, God never intended that he do so. That is why He said that Jesus Christ is to be the husband's example. And His life style for the body of Christ involved unselfishness, humility, and a sacrificial spirit. The average woman will find submission a very easy matter when her husband emulates Christ.

It is true, however, that not every marriage is ideal. For example, there are some unbelieving husbands—as there were in the New Testament. It is in such a marriage that a woman may have to submit under circumstances that are not to her liking. Hopefully, God will use her attitude of willing and loving submission to bring her husband to Christ so that he in turn may eventually love as Christ loved. This is the whole trust of Peter's emphasis in his first Epistle (1 Peter 3:1-6).

A TWENTIETH-CENTURY APPLICATION

Paul is obviously dealing with some special problems among women in the Cretan culture, but as with the qualifications for elders and for men in general, these characteristics we have just considered emerge as supracultural criteria for measuring Christian maturity among women of all time—both old and young.

Lessons for Older Women

1. *To be "reverent in the way they live"*

   One of the major problems among twentieth-century Christians—and since the beginning of the Christian era—is hypocrisy; that is, claiming one thing and living something else. The results are devastating, particularly in the lives of those who know us well. And those who are affected most are younger people. As someone has said, "What you are speaks so loudly I cannot hear what you say." Unfortunately, this is often true among Christians. It does very little good to verbalize something we are not living. Generally speaking, people will not "hear" us under these circumstances; they will only "see" us.

   PERSONAL LIFE-RESPONSE QUESTIONS: To what extent are you living a consistent Christian life style? Are you "worthy of respect"? What do younger women really see when they observe your Christian behavior—your attitude toward your husband, your children, your neighbors, and your enemies?

2. *"Not to be slanderers"*

No one will deny the devastating effects of slander and malicious talk. And all of us, if we are honest with ourselves, will confess that on occasions we have resorted to this kind of behavior. What we must recognize, however, is that in our more sophisticated culture, we sometimes camouflage this kind of verbal attack on others with "sugar-coated" barbs. In fact, we can actually make people feel we are being kind when we are being unkind. In some instances, we may even be rationalizing our own motives.

PERSONAL LIFE-RESPONSE QUESTIONS: Before sharing information about anyone, ask yourself, Will this build the person up? Is it the most merciful thing to say? Have I ever felt envy toward this person? If so, are my motives pure?

SUGGESTIONS: Some people develop a very "cutting" and "piercing" quality in their voice. Ask someone to evaluate your tone of voice and the inflection you use when you communicate with others.

3. *Not "addicted to much wine"*

There is a literal application of Paul's statement to twentieth-century Christians—even in the sophisticated American culture. And with our so-called sophistication has come a "sophistication" in indulgence. The variety of addictive kinds of beverage has multiplied and been made delightfully attractive by multicolor advertisements in magazines, on billboards, and on television. And there are of course other ways in which we can demonstrate intemperance, such as overeating, overspending, oversleeping, overworking—or overindulging in anything!

PERSONAL LIFE-RESPONSE QUESTIONS: Am I *controlled* by any habits that were a part of my non-Christian life style? What are my motives for doing what I do? Are my problems psychological or purely habitual?

For example, some people overeat when they are

under stress. Some people are chain smokers because they are nervous. Some people overdrink because they are anxious. Some people overspend on clothes and items for the home because they feel inferior and insecure.

4. *"To teach what is good"*

As Christians we should always teach what is good, not what is bad or evil, both by our overall life style and by what we say.

PERSONAL LIFE-RESPONSE QUESTIONS: How much is your overall life style reflecting the value systems of Scripture? Have you earned the right to teach others the Bible by first of all applying these truths to your own life?

Lessons for Younger Women

1. *"To love their husbands"*

At least two significant lessons emerge from the study of "biblical love." First, actions are to take precedence over feelings. In fact, in many instances, positive feelings emerge in the process of doing what we know we must do. Second, feelings of affection can be learned. Paul certainly implied this in his statement to Titus. And in most instances, affection is learned through example and experience.

PERSONAL LIFE-RESPONSE QUESTIONS: As a married woman, to what extent are you loving your husband at the "action" level? To what extent are you attempting to learn to love more deeply at the "feeling" level?

NOTE: Some people do not learn to love at the feeling level because they will not deal with feelings of anger and bitterness.

2. *"To love their children"*

Every mother—particularly every young mother—at times experiences feelings of resentment toward her children. These feelings are normal. However, constant resentment indicates a serious problem that needs to be resolved.

PERSONAL LIFE-RESPONSE QUESTIONS: What are you doing to handle the normal feelings of resentment? Do you get sufficient opportunity to get away from these pressures on a periodic basis? Have you shared your deep feelings of frustration and anxiety with your husband and/or a sympathetic friend?

3. *"To be self-controlled"*

A PERSONAL LIFE-RESPONSE QUESTION: Are you controlling your fleshly desire to eat, drink, spend money, and engage in any other carnal habits?

4. *To be "pure"*

Remaining pure is becoming an increasing problem for women in the twentieth-century culture. The new sexual ethic (which is really the old sexual ethic that existed many years ago in Crete) is making it more difficult, especially for young women, to maintain a high level of morality. Movies, magazines, and television shows are blatant in suggestive illegitimate sexual behavior.

A PERSONAL LIFE-RESPONSE QUESTION: To what extent are you maintaining a life of moral purity? Note Paul's exhortation to the Philippians: "Finally, brothers, whatever is true, whatever is noble, whatever is right, whatever is *pure,* whatever is lovely, whatever is admirable—if anything is excellent or praiseworthy—think about such things" (Phil. 4:8).

5. *"To be busy at home"*

A PERSONAL LIFE-RESPONSE QUESTION: The important thing is not whether you are working outside the home, going to school, or pursuing a professional career. Rather, it is this: Are you neglecting your priorities as a wife and/or mother? If you have chosen marriage and homemaking as a way of life, then you have a responsibility to fulfill those obligations if you are indeed to walk in the will of God.

6. *"To be kind"*

PERSONAL LIFE-RESPONSE QUESTIONS: Are

you a kind person, helping others to find fulfillment in life? Are you kind to all people—both Christians and non-Christians?

Note Paul's exhortation: "Let us not become weary in doing good [in being kind], for at the proper time we will reap a harvest if we do not give up. Therefore, as we have opportunity, let us do good [be kind] to all people, especially to those who belong to the family of believers" (Gal. 6:9-10).

7. *"To be subject to their husbands"*

A PERSONAL-RESPONSE QUESTION: How submissive are you to other people in the body of Christ? NOTE: Most women who have difficulty in submitting to their husbands also have difficulty submitting to other people.

Chapter IX

A Profile for Slaves

SOMETHING TO THINK ABOUT

Paul ignored slavery as a social issue.

TRUE or FALSE

If Paul were living today, he would take a different approach to the "racial issue" than he did to "slavery" in the first-century world.

TRUE or FALSE

There is little relationship between being a Christian *slave* in the first-century world and being a Christian *employee* in a free society today.

TRUE or FALSE

A LOOK AT PAUL'S LETTER

2:9 Teach slaves

The Profile

to be subject to their masters in everything, —— 1
to try to please them, —————————— 2
not to talk back to them,
2:10 and
not to steal from them,
but
to show that they can be fully trusted, —— 3

The Purpose

so that in every way they will make the teaching about God our Savior attractive.

WHAT DID PAUL SAY?

A. The Profile

1. Be submissive
2. Attempt to please

3. Develop trust

B. The Purpose

Make the Word of God attractive

WHAT DID PAUL MEAN?

Wherever and whenever the gospel of Christ took root in the hearts of people, it invariably affected a variety of social relationships all over the first-century world. The island of Crete was no exception. At this juncture in his letter, Paul turned his attention to one of the most common social problems facing New Testament Christians—the problem of slavery.

Paul's approach to the evils of this system was unique—and consistent. Rather than attacking the problem peripherally, he struck at its roots. He dealt with the problem in the human heart, specifying clearly the kinds of relationships that should exist among Christians and also between Christians and non-Christians. Nowhere did Paul (or any other New Testament writer) ever demand that slaves be set free. Rather, he dealt with each Christian's attitude and actions—whether slave or free, servant or master—instructing each person *how to live* in any given situation. Over a period of time this unique approach practically eliminated slavery from the New Testament culture. When masters treated their slaves as brothers in Christ and when slaves served their masters as if they were serving the Lord, it was impossible to continue the old system. It eventually disintegrated.

Paul's instructions to Titus regarding the problem at Crete focused on the slaves themselves. However, it must be remembered that he had already clearly delineated a profile for a Christian life style for both men and women of all ages, a life style that certainly included, when applicable, their attitudes and actions toward servants. Paul probably felt it would have been redundant to give any additional instructions just for slave owners. Thus, he concentrated on a life style profile for slaves.

A. The Profile

1. *Be submissive*

"Teach slaves," wrote Paul to Titus, "to be subject to

their masters in everything" (2:9).

It is not possible to reconstruct totally the specific problems facing Christian slaves in the Cretan culture. However, we can draw certain conclusions from what Paul wrote to Titus, one thing being that slaves evidently were not as submissive as they should have been. Perhaps they saw their new freedom in Christ as a rationale for disobedience.

Paul warned against disobedience in this situation, as he did in other situations. When writing to slaves in Ephesus, he said, "Slaves, *obey* your earthly masters with respect and fear, and with sincerity of heart, just as you would *obey* Christ. *Obey* them not only to win their favor when their eye is on you, but like slaves of Christ, doing the will of God from your heart" (Eph. 6:5,6; see also Col. 3:22-25).

We must realize, of course, that when Paul encouraged obedience or submission "in everything," he was assuming that when obedience to man conflicts with obedience to God, we owe our allegiance to God, no matter what the cost.[1] This was the attitude of the apostles when they were given "strict orders not to teach" in the name of Christ by the Sanhedrin in Jerusalem. Their response was that they "must obey God rather than men" (Acts 5:29). They did so, and suffered the consequences.

On the other hand, Paul was also assuming that very few slave owners, even those who were non-Christians, would demand things of their servants that were not right if their slaves had a proper attitude toward their authority and if they did all they could to please their masters. This leads to Paul's next statement.

2. *Attempt to please*

Slaves were to please their masters, wrote Paul, and not "talk back to them" (2:9b).

Here Paul adds another dimension to submission and obedience. It is not only important to do what is asked, but to do it with a *proper spirit* and *attitude*. This generates rapport with an authority figure. On the other hand, a slave who grumbled and "talked back" was openly asking for trouble. Paul was probably directing his comments to slaves in

Philippi when he exhorted, "Do everything without complaining or arguing" (Phil. 2:14).

Inherent in Paul's directive "to *try* to please" their masters is also the concept of *initiative*. This is one of the best ways to win respect and develop credibility. "Don't just do things when asked," implied Paul. Furthermore, "don't just do your work when your masters are watching."

When writing to the Colossians, Paul specified what the basic motivation should be for this kind of commitment:

> Slaves obey your masters in everything; and do it, not only when their eye is on you and to win their favor, but with sincerity of heart and reverence *for ths Lord*. Whatever you do, work at it with all your heart, as working *for the Lord*, not for men, since you know that you will receive an inheritance *from the Lord* as a reward. It is the *Lord Christ* you are serving (Col. 3:22-24).

3. *Develop trust*

There's no quality of life more significant—and personally rewarding—than being trustworthy. For a slave it frequently resulted in a degree of freedom that was almost as beneficial as truly "being free." In conjunction with this quality, Paul warned against stealing, the one activity that destroys trust more than any other thing a person can do.

If Paul was directing his thoughts in this letter to slaves who were now serving Christian masters, it is obvious why he needed to emphasize these qualities of life. The natural tendency for any slave would be to take advantage of the situation. The more benevolent and kind the master became, attempting to reflect Christ in his authority role, the greater the temptation for the slave to abuse these privileges.

This is particularly true in the area of pilfering. It was a common practice among non-Christian slaves. And like all habits, it was difficult to break, even after one became a Christian. Knowing this, Paul told Titus to teach the slaves in Crete who were now Christians to break these old habits: "Teach slaves . . . not to steal . . . but to show they can be fully trusted" (2:10).

One of the most beautiful stories in the New Testament is the account of Onesimus, who was a slave in the household of Philemon. Evidently Paul led this wealthy man and his family to Christ. Frequently under these circumstances slaves also responded to the gospel, especially since they were classified as part of the "household."

Onesimus did not respond, however. He took advantage of the new freedom he must have experienced as he served a Christian master. He gathered up what he could carry with him and escaped, eventually ending up in Rome, where Paul was in prison. In God's providence, Onesimus came in contact with the apostle Paul and was converted to Christ.

In time Paul wrote Philemon and sent the letter via Onesimus. And since Onesimus had no resources, Paul himself took the personal responsibility to pay back what Onesimus had stolen from his master (Philem. 18). This, of course, demonstrates how seriously Paul was committed to honesty and it became a dramatic example to Onesimus that he would never forget.

B. The Purpose

Paul concluded his instructions for slaves by stating the basic reason why they should be submissive to their masters, why they should do all they can to please and why they should develop trust and credibility: "So that in every way they will make the teaching about God our Savior attractive" (2:10).

The basic Greek word *kosmeo,* often translated "adorn" in NASB, is the concept from which we derive the English word "cosmetics." The word was also used in New Testament days to describe the best way to arrange jewels so as to reflect their full beauty.

Viewed from this perspective, what Paul had in mind is quite clear. Slaves were to live in such a way as to *adorn* the Word of God; that is, to make the gospel *attractive*. Their life style was to be like "cosmetics" to the gospel.

The next question is: Attractive to whom? It is impossible

to answer this question specifically. Paul could have had in mind unsaved masters. But it is possible he had in mind both Christian and non-Christian masters, as well as anyone else who looked on. This is what Paul seemed to be referring to when he wrote to Timothy, "All who are under the yoke of slavery should consider their masters worthy of full respect, so that God's name and our teaching may not be slandered." And to cover every situation, Paul added, "Those who have believing masters are not to show less respect for them because they are brothers. Instead, they are to serve them even better, because those who benefit from their service are believers, and dear to them. These are the things you are to teach and urge on them" (1 Tim. 6:1,2).

Whatever Paul's purpose, one thing is clear. He wanted the Cretan slaves to live in such a way so as to enhance the Word of God. Their life style was to conform to what they professed so that all who observed their behavior were attracted to—rather than repulsed by—the teachings of Christ.

A TWENTIETH-CENTURY APPLICATION

For those of us living in the twentieth-century American culture, slavery as it was practiced in the New Testament world is a foreign experience. It is difficult for us even to identify with the problem. However, it is not difficult to identify principles that are applicable to us today in our vocational situations. Indeed, everything Paul said to slaves in Crete applies quite directly to employer–employee relationships in the twentieth-century culture.

Life-Response Questions and Checklist

Following are some questions that grow directly out of this lesson and relate the teachings of Scripture to our lives today. How do you measure up? Check yourself! Give yourself a (+) in your areas of strength. Give yourself a (−) in your areas of weakness. Leave blank those you are not certain about.

1. How *submissive* and *obedient* am I to my employer?

☐ Do I do what is expected of me or am I shirking my responsibilities?
☐ Am I consistently on time for work?
☐ Do I regularly overextend my coffee breaks?
☐ Do I complete assignments as told?
☐ Am I loyal to the company?
☐ Do I listen carefully when I'm told what to do?
☐ Am I thoroughly familiar with the policies of the company?
☐ Others?

NOTE: In twentiety-century culture, most companies allow employees opportunities to state grievances. This is part of our free society. We are not slaves. And if we feel we are being mistreated, we have the privilege of changing jobs. Remember, however, that when stating complaints or when making suggestions, it is often the *way* in which it is done that makes it a Christian or non-Christian approach. It is possible to disagree and still maintain an attitude of submissiveness and obedience.

2. Do I do all I can to *please* my employer?

☐ Do I serve my employer as if I am serving the Lord?
☐ Do I serve just as well when he is not observing my work as I do when he is observing my work?
☐ Do I initiate projects within the guidelines of the company?
☐ Do I do everything I can to make my employer look good to others?
☐ Am I simply "punching a clock," or am I willing in emergencies to put in extra time, even though it may not affect my salary?
☐ Am I "goal oriented" or simply "job oriented?"
☐ Others?

NOTE: What are some of the dangers in the average twentieth-century place of business when an employee does all he can to please his employer? How might this be misinterpreted? What can a Christian do to avoid this misinterpretation and yet be true to the Scriptures?

3. Am I doing all I can to develop *credibility* and *trust?*

- ☐ Am I honest in all my activities?
- ☐ Do I illegitimately use company time for my own selfish interests?
- ☐ Do I illegitimately use company equipment, materials, and other resources for personal needs?
- ☐ Do I always tell the truth, both by what I say and by what I do not say?
- ☐ Others?

NOTE: Some employers have various policies and guidelines regarding employee privileges and benefits. Make sure you are within these guidelines. If in doubt, ask for clarification from your immediate superior.

REMEMBER: It is better to be more "conservative" than "liberal" in interpreting these guidelines.

4. As an employee, how much does my Christian life style make the Word of God attractive to both Christians and non-Christians? (Evaluate your life in the light of the following biblical injunctions.)

- ☐ "Make it your ambition to lead a quiet life, to mind your own business and to work with your hands, just as we told you, so that your daily life may win the respect of outsiders and so that you will not be dependent on anybody." (1 Thess. 4:11-12)
- ☐ "So whether you eat or drink or whatever you do, do it all for the glory of God. Do not cause anyone to stumble, whether Jews, Greeks or the church

of God—even as I try to please everybody in every way. For I am not seeking my own good but the good of many, so that they may be saved. Follow my example, as I follow the example of Christ." (1 Cor. 10:31 – 11:1)

☐ "Live such good lives among the pagans that, though they accuse you of doing wrong, they may see your good deeds and glorify God on the day he visits us." (1 Peter 2:12)

☐ "Be wise in the way you act toward outsiders; make the most of every opportunity. Let your conversation be always full of grace, seasoned with salt, so that you may know how to answer everyone." (Col. 4:5-6)

☐ "But in your hearts acknowledge Christ as the holy Lord. Always be prepared to give an answer to everyone who asks you to give the reason for the hope that you have. But do this with gentleness and respect, keeping a clear conscience, so that those who speak maliciously against your good behavior in Christ may be ashamed of their slander." (1 Peter 3:15-16)

☐ What other Scriptures could you add to this list?

NOTE

[1]There is a difference of opinion among New Testament scholars regarding the punctuation in the Greek text in Titus 2:9. Some translators associate "in everything" with the phrase "to try to please them." This is true in the King James, which reads, "Exhort servants to be obedient unto their own masters, and *to please them well in all things*." Obviously the translators of the NIV disagree, as do those of the NASB. It really doesn't matter which view is held, since Paul made a similar statement in Colossians 3:22 and there is no question as to what he had in mind. It is very clear that Paul was saying that slaves should obey their masters "in everything."

Chapter X

A Christian Life Style—and God's Grace

SOMETHING TO THINK ABOUT

What should be the motivating force that causes a Christian to live a godly life style? Can you identify that force in *your* life?

A LOOK AT PAUL'S LETTER

God's Grace—and Redemption

2:11 For the grace of God
that brings salvation ———————— 1
has appeared to all men. ———— 2

God's Grace—and Purification

2:12 It teaches us
to say "No" to
ungodliness ———————— 1
and
worldly passions, ———————— 2
and
to live self-controlled, ———————— 3
upright ———————— 4
and
godly lives in this present age, — 5

God's Grace—and Glorification

2:13 while we wait for the blessed hope—
the glorious appearing
of our great God and Savior, Jesus Christ,
2:14 who gave himself for us ———————— A3
to redeem us from all wickedness
and
to purify for himself a people that are his very own,
eager to do what is good.

WHAT DID PAUL SAY?

A. God's Grace—and Redemption (2:11, 14a)

1. What is it? (God's unmerited favor)
2. For whom is it? (all men)
3. How has it been revealed? (through Jesus Christ)

B. God's Grace—and Purification (2:12, 14b)

It teaches us:

1. To *avoid* ungodliness

2. To *avoid* worldly passions

3. To *live* self-controlled lives
4. To *live* upright lives

5. To *live* godly lives

C. God's Grace—and Glorification (2:13)

WHAT DID PAUL MEAN?

We come to a point in Paul's letter to Titus where he made several profound statements that are both a *continuation* of what he has just said in the previous paragraph and a *summation* of what he has written about in the beginning of this Epistle. This literary technique certainly reflects Paul's genius as a writer, but it also demonstrates that he was inspired by the Holy Spirit as he penned this letter. Let's look specifically at what he said in these verses and see how these statements relate to both the immediate and the overall context.

A. God's Grace—and Redemption (2:11,14a)

The theme of this paragraph stands out clearly as the "grace of God." But before we can understand clearly what Paul was saying, we must understand the term *grace*. What is grace? How is it defined biblically? Most Bible scholars agree that it generally refers to God's unmerited favor toward mankind, but especially toward those who respond to his infinite love through Jesus Christ.

Paul reminded Titus, first of all, that it was the "grace of God that *brings salvation*."[1] Put another way, Paul was referring to *redemption*, which he clarifies later by stating that Christ gave Himself to "*redeem us* from all wickedness" (2:14). Jesus Christ paid the ransom for our sin in order to set us *free* from sin now (Rom. 6:5-7) and eternally (Eph. 1:13,14).

Paul then described those who are *recipients* of God's grace—"the grace of God that brings salvation has appeared to *all men*." Through "the grace of God" Jesus Christ tasted death "for everyone" (Heb. 2:9). He died for the sins of "the world" (John 3:16).

Paul's statement that God's grace has appeared to "all men" grows naturally out of his previous comments regarding slaves. Thus Paul was no doubt referring to "all kinds and classes of men." Obviously, he was not saying that God's grace in Jesus Christ has appeared to all men in the sense that all men have heard about it. Rather, this grace is *available* to *all people*—no matter what our status or position in life. In other words, because of God's grace, "there is neither Jew nor Greek, slave nor free, male nor female, for [we] are all one in Christ Jesus" (Gal. 3:28).

There is one other important question that must be answered before we go further—how has this grace, this unmerited favor of God, been revealed? If it is available to all men, how has it been manifested? Paul answers this question specifically in 2:14: Jesus Christ "gave himself." God's grace was certainly obvious in the Old Testament—when He chose Abraham, when He chose the nation Israel to be His own special people, and when He continued to love them and bless them in spite of their disobedience. This, indeed, was God's grace. But it reaches its fullest manifestation when Christ came into the world. Thus John wrote, "The word became flesh and lived for a while among us. We have seen his glory, the glory of the one and only Son, who came from the Father, full of *grace* and truth" (John 1:14).

Jesus Christ was the perfect embodiment of God's grace. He was the sinless Son of God who died on the cross to become the perfect sacrifice for sin. His life, His death, His resurrection, and His ascension all reveal God's grace.

The grace of God, then, has appeared to all men in Christ, both by what He did and by what He said. And that grace continues to be clearly evident to us today through the written record of Christ as we find it in the Bible. Just as Christ taught men who He was and why He came, so the message of the Bible, God's Word, continues to reveal God's grace to all people, no matter what their race, color, creed, or position in life. He came to be the Savior of "all men."

B. God's Grace—and Purification (2:12,14b)

God's grace, though it is available to all people, is operative only in the life of the person who responds to the message of redemption. First, a person receives eternal life as a result of God's grace. As Paul wrote to the Ephesians, "For it is by *grace* you have been saved, *through faith*—and this not from yourselves, it is the gift of God—not by works, so that no one can boast'' (Eph. 2:8-9). Second, God's grace (His unmerited favor through Christ) continues to operate in a believer's life. Thus Paul wrote to Titus that God's grace ''teaches us.'' How can this be?

First of all, people who have truly experienced God's grace and understand that it is His unmerited favor toward us, —toward all of us who deserve the very opposite—will respond by conforming their lives to Christ's life. This was Paul's appeal in Romans 12:1,2: ''I urge you, . . . *in view of God's mercy* [his unmerited favor], to offer yourselves as living sacrifices, holy and pleasing to God—which is your spiritual worship. Do not conform any longer to the pattern of this world, but be transformed by the renewing of your mind'' (Rom. 12:1,2a). Can we do less than obediently respond to God's grace when we *understand* that grace?

This is why it is important to teach people the true significance of God's grace. Some believe that to emphasize salvation by grace apart from works will cause people to become more careless in how they live. Not so—if they indeed are taught the real meaning of grace. A person who has truly been converted and who understands clearly what it cost Christ to save him will respond to God's love. Though we are human and certainly will sin, we will also respond to God's grace in our lives. This is true because ''we are God's workmanship, created in Christ Jesus to *do good works,* which God prepared in advance for us to do'' (Eph. 2:10). This is why James emphasized that true faith will produce works (James 2:17). And this is also why Paul in this very passage under consideration wrote that Christ ''gave himself for us,'' not only ''to redeem us'' but also ''to *purify* for himself a people that are his very own, *eager to do what is good*'' (Titus 2:14). A Christian, then, who truly understands God's grace in saving him will desire to conform his life to the will of God.

This leads us to a second way in which God's grace ''teaches us.'' For it to teach us, it must be taught to us; that is, Christians must understand God's grace. This is not any more automatic than conversion is. We can respond to the gospel only when we *know* that Christ died and rose again for us. And we can respond to His grace in our Christian lives only when we *know* how He wants us to live. This is why Paul and other writers of Scripture teach both what Christ has done for us and *how* we should live in view of what he has done.

Paul's letter to Titus is, of course, a dramatic example of teaching people what is expected of Christians who have been redeemed by God's grace. In this letter Paul spells out point by point, from beginning to end, those qualities of life that should accompany salvation. And just as God's grace in salvation is available to all kinds and classes of people, so Paul spells out a Christian life style for all kinds and classes of people.

In the paragraph before us, however, Paul brings together in a succinct form what God's grace should be teaching us as Christians. In a sense Paul is asking, "How can I summarize all I've said about Christian living?" and then gives his answer in Titus 2:11-14. He answered the question first from a negative and then a positive perspective. Grace teaches us, he wrote:

1. *To avoid ungodliness*

"Ungodliness" is a broad term. It includes everything that a person does without taking God into account. An ungodly person focuses on himself. He does not recognize or acknowledge his dependence on God as the creator and sustainer of all life. His philosophy is man-centered, not God-centered. The false teachers best exemplified this kind of thinking.

In today's world ungodliness can be illustrated by two major philosophies —*naturalism* and *supernaturalism.* A naturalist is characterized by "ungodliness," since he does not take God into account in explaining life and the universe. A Christian—whether man or woman, young or old, slave or free—who understands God's grace and who is taught by it should avoid this kind of thinking. Putting it more directly, he should reject ungodliness as a true philosophy of life.

2. *To avoid worldly passions*

"Worldly passions" or "lusts" represent the *results* of an ungodly life. They constitute not only a "way of thinking" but a specific life style. A person who engages in this kind of behavior seeks those things that cater to fleshly appetites regardless of God's laws. He is a materialist and a sensualist. He does not seek first the kingdom of God and His righteousness, but rather all that is in the world that will satisfy his carnal and selfish desires.

Again, the false teachers illustrate this kind of life style. Their motive was dishonest gain. They were rebellious against God's will. To them nothing was pure. Even one of their own philosophers called them "Liars, evil brutes, lazy gluttons." Paul agreed! He said they were "detestable, disobedient and unfit for doing anything good" (Titus 1:10-16).

Paul next turned to a positive point of view, in a sense giving a reverse perspective. Grace teaches us, he wrote.

3. *To live self-controlled lives*

For the fifth time in this letter we encounter this quality of life. It represents the opposite of allowing our appetites and passions to run wild. It means bringing our human feelings and desires into conformity with God's expectations.

4. *To live upright lives*

We have looked also at this quality of life earlier in our study. Paul used the word *upright* along with the word *holy* to describe the qualifications for an elder (1:8). As stated earlier, a Christian who is living this kind of life is exemplifying the life of Jesus Christ.

5. *To live godly lives*

It goes without saying—though I am saying it—that a "godly" life is the opposite of an "ungodly" life. A godly person orders his life around Jesus Christ. His total decision-making process has as its focus God's will and ways, whether in his personal life, his family life, his church life, his business life, or his recreational life. Whether he eats or drinks, or whatever he does, he does it all for the glory of God (1 Cor. 10:31). Paraphrasing an Old Testament writer, a

Christian who is godly trusts in the Lord with all his heart, does not lean on his own understanding, and acknowledges God in all his ways (Prov. 3:5,6).[2]

C. God's Grace—and Glorification

Before Jesus Christ returned to heaven He promised He would come again to take all of His children to be with Him (John 14:1-3). It will happen "in a flash, in the twinkling of an eye," and when it happens "we shall be changed" (1 Cor. 15:52). Then Jesus Christ "will transform our lowly bodies so that they will be like His glorious body" (Phil. 3:21).

In the meantime, however, we are to be in the process of being changed, even in our earthly bodies. As we have seen from this passage of Scripture, the grace of Christ teaches us to become like Him, even before we are ultimately glorified. Though we can never reach perfection on this earth and though we will stumble and fall and sin against the Lord, yet we are to "be transformed by the renewing of [our] mind" (Rom. 12:2). This clearly is a process. And part of our motivation to "not conform any longer to the pattern of this world, but be transformed," is the fact that He *is* coming again. Thus John wrote, "Dear friends, now we are children of God, and what we will be has not yet been made known. But we know that when he appears, we shall be like him, for we shall see him as he is. *Everyone who has this hope in him purifies himself, just as he is pure*" (John 3:2,3).

This was Paul's message to Titus and to the Cretan Christians. The basic motivation for this kind of changing life style was to be His grace—His unmerited favor toward them in redeeming them and giving them such a glorious hope. Furthermore, they should desire to please Him and not be ashamed at His coming (1 John 2:28). After all, He "gave himself for us to redeem us from all wickedness and to purify for himself a people that are his very own, eager to do what is good" (Titus 2:14). The least we can do as Christians is to offer Him "ourselves as living sacrifices, holy and pleasing to God"—an act of "spiritual worship" (Rom. 12:1). Anything less is an attempt to take advantage of His grace.

A TWENTIETH-CENTURY APPLICATION

There are at least two major concerns emerging from this study—concerns that ought to capture the attention of every twentieth-century Christian. First, what is an adequate Christian philosophy of life? Second, what about people who profess to be Christians but do not live lives that reflect these qualities?

A Christian Philosophy of Life

Behind every individual's *way of life* stands a *way of thinking*. In other words, every person's particular life style reflects a certain philosophy of life. True, many people may have difficulty verbalizing their philosophy of life in a succinct and coherent fashion, but it is there nevertheless.

In Titus 2:11-14 Paul treats the basic ingredients that should make up every Christian's philosophy of life, which in turn should mold his personal life style. At the center of that philosophy should be an understanding and appreciation of God's grace toward us and the glorious position we have in Christ (see illustration).

Like all people, we were under the curse of God's law, for, as Paul stated in Galatians, "Clearly no one is justified before God by the law" (Gal. 3:11). However, in an act of love unparalleled in the universe, "Christ redeemed us from the curse of the law by becoming a curse for us" (Gal. 3:13). He died for our sins and rose again, ascended to heaven until that special day when He will return to take us to live with Him forever. At that moment we will be completely transformed into His likeness, receiving glorified bodies. God's grace in redeeming us set us eternally free from His judgment, not only while we live our lives here on earth but for all eternity.

A clear understanding of God's grace will make an indelible impression on every believer. There is no way we can ignore such love. It will inevitably affect our life style. It will create within us a desire to please God, to conform our lives to His will here and now. Thus Paul exhorted the Ephesians to "*be imitators of God* . . . and live a life of love, just as

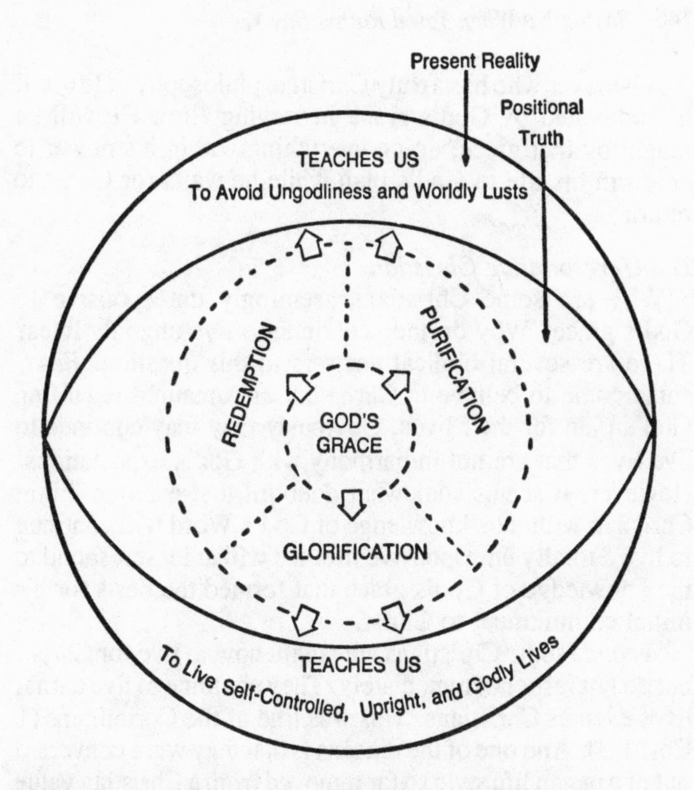

Christ loved us and gave himself up for us as a fragrant offering and sacrifice to God'' (Eph. 5:1,2).

Paul himself stands out as a dynamic example of a man motivated by God's grace. Of all New Testament Christians, he perhaps best understood God's grace and was affected by it most. This seems obvious in his writings and especially in the following statement he made to Timothy: ''Even though I was once a blasphemer and a persecutor and a violent man, I was shown mercy because I acted in ignorance and unbelief. *The grace of our Lord* was poured out on me abundantly, along with the faith and love that are in Christ Jesus'' (1 Tim. 1:13,14). Paul never got over the impact of God's grace in his life. It motivated him to live every moment for God's honor and glory. His basic desire was to please the One who loved him when he was anything but worthy of that love.

A believer who has a truly Christian philosophy of life will be motivated by God's grace in serving Him. He will be taught by that grace, doing everything within his power to conform his life to God's plan while he waits for Christ to return.

The Unresponsive Christian

Why are some Christians seemingly unresponsive to God's grace? Why do they continue to live ungodly lives? There are several biblical answers to this question. *First,* some come to believe in Christ but are untaught regarding God's plan for their lives. Obviously they may continue to live lives that are not in harmony with God's expectations. However, it seems somewhat doubtful that even an infant Christian without a knowledge of God's Word will continue to live a totally unresponsive life. He will at least respond to the knowledge of God's grace that formed the basis for his initial commitment to Christ.

Second, some Christians are taught how to live for Christ, but do not respond immediately. They continue to live carnal lives even as Christians. This was true of the Corinthians (1 Cor. 1-3). And one of the reasons is that they were converted out of a pagan life style so far removed from a Christian value system that it took time to make a transition. But eventually they *did* respond to the Word of God. They could not ignore God's grace (2 Cor. 7:8-16).

Third, some people profess to be Christians but they have never truly been converted to Christ. They are "Christian" in name only. They do not grow spiritually, since there is no new life to begin with.

The apostle John spoke to this issue rather pointedly in his first Epistle: "We can be sure we know him if we obey his commands. The man who says, 'I know him,' but does not do what he commands is a liar, and the truth is not in him. But if anyone obeys his word, God's love is truly made complete in him. This is how we know we are in him: Whoever claims to live in him must walk as Jesus did" (1 John 2:3-6).

A PERSONAL LIFE RESPONSE

Following are some questions to help you evaluate your philosophy of life.

1. To what extent are you affected by God's grace? Does it influence your total life style? Are you responding to God's grace out of appreciation or duty? To what extent do you even understand God's grace? What are you doing to understand *more* of God's grace?

2. How would you classify yourself as an individual:
   - ☐ A Christian who has been taught very little about God's grace and His plan for my life.
   - ☐ A Christian who knows a lot about God's love and grace but who has taken advantage of that grace and responded very little.
   - ☐ A person who thought I was a Christian but now I am unsure because there has been very little fruit in my life.

In the light of this lesson from the Word of God, write out an action step you need to take immediately in order to conform your life to God's perfect will:

____

____

____

CAUTION: God does not expect perfection in this life. That is impossible. But He does expect us to grow spiritually and to become more and more like His Son Jesus Christ.

NOTES

[1]Paul was probably using the word *salvation* in this instance to refer to the complete process of salvation, which is spelled out in Romans 8:29-30: "For those God foreknew he also predestined to be conformed to the likeness of his Son, that he might be the firstborn among many brothers. And those he predestined, he also called; those he called, he also justified; those he justified, he also glorified."

[2]Notice the correlation between the qualities Paul states for elders in Titus 1:7,8 and the summary qualifications for *all* Christians in Titus 2:12. This correlation is obvious not only in the specific nature of each quality, but also in the grammatical structure. In both instances Paul gives a negative perspective first and then a positive perspective. Furthermore, the qualities in each of these categories are also quite similar in meaning. For example, in the qualities of an elder Paul states that "He must be blameless, *not* overbearing, *not* quick-tempered, *not* given to much wine, *not* violent, *not* pursuing dishonest gain." In Titus 2:12 Paul states that God's grace teaches us to "say 'No' to ungodliness and worldly passions," two concepts that summarize rather well the characteristics we are to say "no" to in Titus 1:7.

The same observation can be made about the positive qualities in Titus 1:8. There is an even more direct correlation between the six qualities listed there and those positive qualities listed in Titus 2:12. In essence, then, Paul summarizes for all Christians in Titus 2:12 what he spells out specifically for elders in Titus 1:7,8.

Chapter XI

A Christian Life Style—and the Non-Christian Community

SOMETHING TO THINK ABOUT

Does a Christian ever have the right to disobey government leaders?

☐ YES

☐ NO

☐ UNCERTAIN

A LOOK AT PAUL'S LETTER

A Summation

2:15 These, then, are the things you should teach.
Encourage
and
rebuke with all authority. —— 1
Do not let anyone despise you. —— 2

A Reminder

3:1 Remind the people to be subject to rulers — a
and
authorities,
to be obedient, —— b
to be ready to do whatever is good, — c
(a–c: 1)

3:2 to slander no one, —— a
to be peaceable —— b
and
considerate, —— c
and
to show true humility toward all men. – d
(a–d: 2)

WHAT DID PAUL SAY?

A. A Summation

Teach all classes of people:

1. With authority

2. With confidence

B. A Reminder

Review behavioral expectations

1. Toward government authorities
   a. Be submissive
   b. Be obedient

   c. Be willing
2. Toward all non-Christians
   a. Slander no one
   b. Be peaceable

   c. Be considerate

   d. Be humble

WHAT DID PAUL MEAN?

A. A Summation

Paul introduced this section of his letter (chapter 2) by instructing Titus to *"teach what is in accord with sound doctrine"* (2:1); that is, to emphasize those qualities and characteristics for all classes of men and women that should accompany and reflect sound teaching. He then proceeded to spell out paragraph by paragraph what in actuality should accompany sound doctrine in the lives of older men, older women, younger women, young men, and slaves.

After giving a rather extended list of qualities, Paul captured the essence of this "sound doctrine" that formed the basis of his appeal for a godly life style—God's grace in Christ Jesus, which has provided redemption for all men, now and eternally. And, continued Paul, this grace—this unmerited favor towards all men—*"teaches us"* (those who respond to God's grace by faith) to live lives that conform to God's gift of eternal life.

Before moving on to another aspect of Christian living, Paul summarized his exhortation to Titus. He actually ended this section where he began: *"These, then, are the things you should teach"* (2:15a). What "things"? Those qualities of life that should characterize every person who has responded to God's grace in Jesus Christ.

But in the summation Paul, as he often did in his "summaries," elaborated on some points. He wanted to exhort Titus to communicate these spiritual concepts, with a sense of *authority* and *confidence*.

1. *He was to teach with authority*

The word *authority* reminds us of Paul's opening words in this Epistle where he referred to his apostolic calling and the fact that the "preaching entrusted" to him was by direct "command [or authority] of God."[1] Part of that authoritative message entrusted to Paul was a "knowledge of the truth that *leads to godliness*" (Titus 1:2,3). In other words, Paul had just spelled out clearly and in detail to Titus what he had learned by direct revelation about a Christian life style. And he wanted Titus to teach these truths to others with the same degree of authority as if he had received them directly from God. For indeed, this profile for a Christian life style for all classes of people came directly from God, though Titus had learned these truths from the apostle Paul.

This was also why Paul wrote to Timothy, saying, "And *the things you have heard me say* in the presence of many witnesses entrust to *reliable* men who will also be *qualified* to teach others" (2 Tim. 2:2). In other words, anyone who understood God's truth and who had demonstrated reliability in their own Christian life style was "qualified" and "competent" to teach others God's truth with a sense of authority. And certainly this applied to Titus. Paul left him in Crete because he was a man of God who had held "firmly to the trustworthy message as it had been taught," and this in turn gave him the right to "encourage others by sound doctrine and refute those who oppose[d] it" (Titus 1:9). This is why Paul summarized this section on a Christian life style by saying, "These, then, are the things you should teach. *Encourage* and *rebuke* with *all authority*" (Titus 2:15).[2]

2. *He was to teach with confidence*

Following Paul's injunction to Titus to "encourage and rebuke *with all authority,*" he concluded his summation by stating that he should not let anyone despise him; that is, he should not let anyone treat him scornfully and look down on him. In essence this is what Paul stated to Timothy: "Don't let anyone look down on you [despise you] because you are young . . ." (1 Tim. 4:12a).

Titus had no reason to let others "put him down." He could speak with confidence. He was standing foursquare on God's trustworthy message. No one had the right to make fun of him, to intimidate him, to undermine his sense of security. He had no reason to be "ashamed" (Rom. 1:16). Like Paul, he was "Christ's ambassador (2 Cor. 5:20).

B. A Reminder

Paul's next injunction to Titus must have been a "review" of some of the things he had already taught the Cretan

Christians while he was still with them. Consequently, he instructed Titus to *remind* the people" of certain things (3:1); that is, to "bring certain things to their remembrance."

1. *Their attitudes and actions toward governing authorities*

First Paul was concerned about their behavior in relation to "rulers and authorities." No doubt they had originally rebelled against the government. This would not be an uncommon reaction on the part of a non-Christian Cretan. If they were generally classified as "liars, evil brutes," and "lazy gluttons" (1:12), we can easily imagine how this would affect their attitudes toward authority figures. And, as we have seen, a non-Christian life style can very easily transfer over into a person's "new life" in Christ. This is why Paul and other New Testament writers had to continually exhort New Testament Christians "to live a life worthy of the calling" they had received (Eph. 4:1).

Paul enumerated three basic behavioral expectations for Christians toward government officials. First, they were "to be *subject*" to them—not a new concept in this letter, nor in other New Testament Epistles. "Subjection" or "submission" involves subjecting oneself to another authority figure, accepting advice and counsel, and, if necessary, yielding to another person's admonitions and commands.

Obedience is the second word Paul used to describe what a Christian's actions should be to these Cretan leaders. It is difficult to differentiate between "submission" and "obedience." Certainly the two words together reinforce the importance of doing what is expected of a good citizen.

However, Paul, as he so often did, added balance to these instructions when he told Titus to remind the believers "to *be ready* to do whatever is good." With this statement Paul was doing two things, First, he was emphasizing, at least by implication, that there are times when all Christians, like the apostles in Jerusalem, "must obey God rather than men" (Acts 5:29). We are to do "good," not "evil." But on the other hand, Paul was emphasizing that if Christians are "*ready* to do whatever is good," it will quickly reduce, or perhaps eliminate, the times government leaders will ask them to do what is "not good." Proper Christian attitudes and actions toward most non-Christians—particularly authority figures—will work wonders in most cultures in creating an environment that is free from harassment. This is why Paul stated in his Roman letter:

> Everyone must submit himself to the governing authorities, for there is no authority except that which God has established. The authorities that exist have been established by God. Consequently, he who rebels against the authority is rebelling against what God has instituted, and those who do so will bring judgment on themselves. For rulers hold no terror for those *who do right*, but for those *who do wrong*. Do you want to be *free from fear* of the one in authority? Then do *what is right* and *he will commend you* (Rom. 13:1-3).

Understand of course that government authorities who have been established by God do not necessarily always do the will of God. But what Paul is emphasizing is that one of the quickest ways to keep them from unnecessarily doing evil things to Christians is to respect them and submit to them whenever possible. And if a Christian views government officials as truly being "established by God," then they will submit "not only because of possible punishment, but also because of conscience" (Rom. 13:5).

One of the areas in which New Testament Christians sometimes resisted government authorities was their refusal to "pay taxes." Some refused to pay "respect" and "honor," feeling that by showing honor to men they were violating their allegiance to God. Not so, wrote Paul to the Romans. "Give everyone what you owe him: If you owe taxes, pay taxes; if revenue, then revenue; if respect, then respect; if honor, then honor" (Rom. 13:7).

2. *Toward all non-Christians*

Paul turned his attention next to the behavior Cretan Christians should exhibit toward *all* non-Christians. He outlined four qualities of life.

First, they were to *"slander no one."* That is, they were not to use abusive language and speak reproachfully of non-Christians, no matter what the occasion. They might disagree with a non-Christian's behavior, but they were never to allow "unwholesome talk" to come out of their mouths (Eph. 4:29). Their conversation was to "be always full of grace, seasoned with salt," in order that they might "know how to answer everyone" (Col. 4:5,6).

Second, they were "to be *peaceable,*" or "uncontentious." Interestingly, this is a mark of maturity specified for an elder in Paul's letter to Timothy (1 Tim. 3:2). The Cretan believers were not to go around stirring up trouble in the non-Christian community. Rather, they were to do everything they could to create peace without violating their Christian convictions.

Third, they were "to be *considerate.*" Again, this is a quality specified for an elder (1 Tim. 3:3). It refers to demonstrating a spirit of "gentleness" toward unbelievers. This kind of attitude is more explicitly explained by Paul in his second letter to Timothy when he said, "And the Lord's servant must not quarrel; instead, he must be kind to *everyone,* able to teach, not resentful. Those who oppose him he must gently instruct, in the hope that God will give them a change of heart leading them to a knowledge of the truth" (2 Tim. 2:24-25).

Fourth, they were "to show true *humility* toward all men." Here Paul was probably referring to being courteous. They were not to treat non-Christians with an attitude of superiority, pride, and arrogance. As we will see in our next chapters, these attitudes ought not to characterize our lives as Christians, for it was only because of God's love, kindness, and mercy toward us that we have been saved (3:3-5). Therefore, we have no right to boast about our position in Jesus Christ.

In summary, these four qualities of life help make it possible for a Christian to "have a good reputation with outsiders" (1 Tim. 3:7). Even those who despise us and abuse us and accuse us of doing wrong may see our good deeds and eventually "glorify God" (1 Peter 2:12). For as Peter also wrote, "It is God's will that by doing *good* you should silence the ignorant talk of foolish men" (1 Peter 2:15). And furthermore, wrote Peter, "Always be prepared to give an answer to everyone who asks you to give the reason for the hope that you have. But do this with *gentleness* and *respect,* keeping a clear conscience, so that those who speak maliciously against your *good behavior in Christ* may be ashamed of their slander" (1 Peter 3:15,15).

A TWENTIETH-CENTURY APPLICATION

There are two important areas where this passage touches our lives as twentieth-century Christians.

1. *We, too, have an authoritative message to communicate to all men.* We need not apologize nor should we ever be ashamed. Though not all men will receive it (including some Christians), we must not allow ourselves to be intimidated. When we are speaking God's truth and some reject it, they are not rejecting us, but God.

   However, there are several things about our communication that we must constantly evaluate. Some Christians find their words rejected (and themselves) because of the way they communicate. A dogmatic, insensitive attitude will usually bring a negative response on the part of most people. There are exceptions to this of course because some people are so emotionally sick they want people to dominate and control them. But in general, this is not true.

   The Scriptures are clear. We can be *authoritative* without being "authoritarian." We can know what we believe and communicate it without reflecting a "know-it-all" attitude. This is a constant challenge for every Christian.

   Remember too that some Christians become authoritarian because they are insecure in what they believe. When their faith is challenged, they become defensive and argumentative. This we must also guard against. In fact, this is what Paul was referring to in 2 Timothy 2:23-26.

Another thing we must be sure of when we "encourage and rebuke with all authority" is that we are speaking the truth. It is possible to misinterpret Scripture and teach it incorrectly. If we do, we will discover resistance, particularly on the part of sincere, thinking Christians.

Again, there are exceptions, for there are some people who want to hear false doctrine, particularly when it presents a "form of godliness" but denies "its power" (2 Tim. 3:5). In this case we must not interpret "acceptance" of our message as meaning we are correct in our interpretation of Scripture.

All of this indicates the importance of being a part of a functioning body of believers. All of us are needed to help one another speak "the truth in love." When we do, Paul says, "we will in all things grow up into him who is the Head, that is, Christ. From him the whole body, joined and held together by every supporting ligament, grows and builds itself up in love, as each part does its work" (Eph. 4:15-16).

2. *Second, every Christian must evaluate his or her attitude toward non-Christians*—first toward governing authorities, some of whom are not Christians, and second, toward all unbelievers. The following questions will help you.

In my attitudes and actions toward governing authorities:

(1) Am I characterized by an attitude of *submissiveness?* For example, what is my attitude to a police officer when I am caught violating the speed limit?

(2) Am I characterized by an attitude of *obedience?* For example, do I obey speed laws? Do I pay taxes when they are due? Do I honor and respect government officials?

NOTE: It is true that some men in government are not worthy of respect. However, this never justifies a disrespectful attitude on the part of a

Christian. We must always speak "the *truth* in love"—no matter who is involved.

(3) Am I characterized by an attitude of *willingness to do what is good?* For example, do I do things only after being reprimanded by authority figures?

(4) Do I pray for government officials (1 Tim. 2:1)?

In my attitude toward non-Christians generally:

(1) Do I ever slander non-Christians? For example, how do I treat non-Christians in the office where I work? What do I say behind their back?

NOTE: It is necessary sometimes to "speak out" on issues of right or wrong. But it is possible to do so without slandering another person. It is true that it may cause difficulty and misunderstanding, but never let it happen because of anger, resentment, and insensitive actions and attitudes.

(2) Do I do everything I can to live in peace and harmony with non-Christians without compromising *true* Christian standards?

NOTE: Some Christians need to learn how to be "in the world" without "being a part of it." "Separation from the world" is not "isolation."

(3) Am I considerate and kind to all non-Christians?

(4) Am I characterized by an attitude of courtesy, humility, and sensitivity?

NOTES

[1]Here Paul used the same Greek word as in Titus 2:15. In 1:3 the message entrusted to Paul was given "by the *command* [*epitagee*] of God our Savior"; in 2:15 Paul instructed Titus to "encourage and rebuke with all *authority* [*epitagee*]."

[2]Note that these words Paul used in Titus 2:15 *(encourage* and *rebuke)* were the same basic words he used in 1:7 to describe the function of an elder who was holding "firmly to the trustworthy message as it [had] been taught" (1:9).

Chapter XII

Why Christians Should Be Sensitive to Non-Christians

SOMETHING TO THINK ABOUT

Check those attitudes and feelings you have most often toward non-Christians who are living in open and flagrant sin.

- ☐ Anger
- ☐ Anxiety
- ☐ Sorrow
- ☐ Jealousy
- ☐ Sympathy
- ☐ Compassion
- ☐ Sadness
- ☐ Resentment
- ☐ Other ________

A LOOK AT PAUL'S LETTER

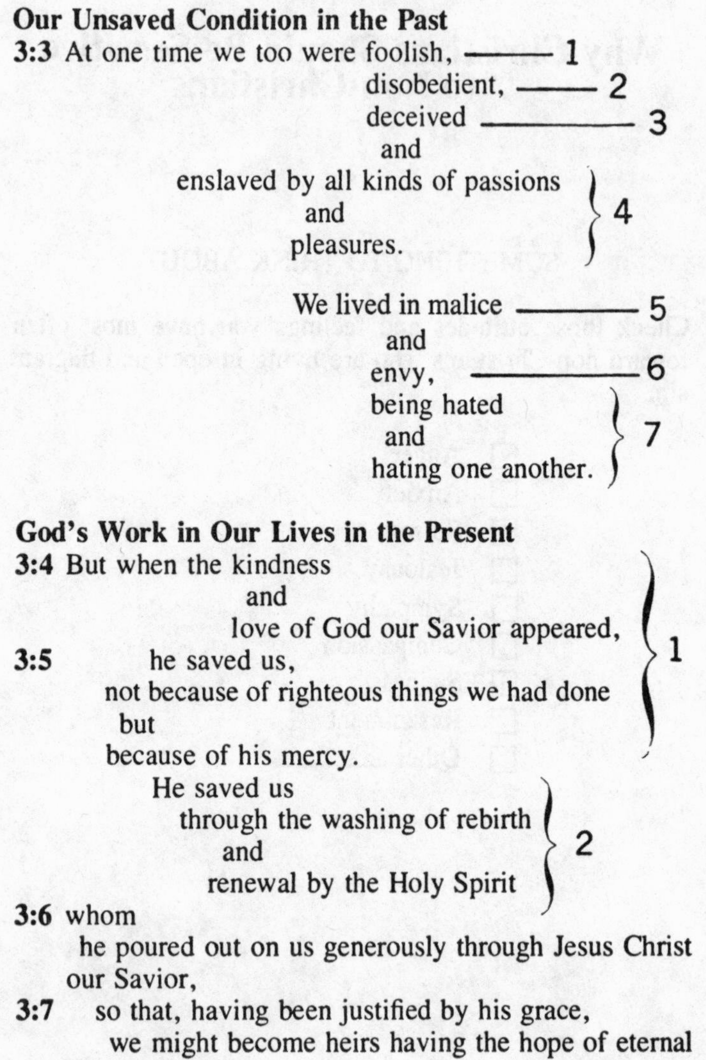
Our Unsaved Condition in the Past

3:3 At one time we too were foolish, —— 1
disobedient, —— 2
deceived —— 3
and
enslaved by all kinds of passions and pleasures. } 4

We lived in malice —— 5
and
envy, —— 6
being hated and hating one another. } 7

God's Work in Our Lives in the Present

3:4 But when the kindness
and
love of God our Savior appeared,
3:5 he saved us,
not because of righteous things we had done
but
because of his mercy. } 1

He saved us
through the washing of rebirth
and
renewal by the Holy Spirit } 2

3:6 whom
he poured out on us generously through Jesus Christ our Savior,

3:7 so that, having been justified by his grace,
we might become heirs having the hope of eternal life.

WHAT DID PAUL SAY?

We should understand non-Christians and respond to them properly because of:

A. Our Unsaved Condition in the Past

1. We were foolish
2. We were disobedient
3. We were deceived
4. We were enslaved
   a. By passions
   b. By pleasures
5. We lived in malice

6. We lived in envy
7. We lived in hatred

B. God's Work in Our Lives in the Present

1. We were saved by grace

2. We are being renewed by the Holy Spirit

WHAT DID PAUL MEAN?

In the previous paragraph in this letter Paul instructed Titus to remind the Cretan Christians to behave properly toward all non-Christians, but particularly toward authority figures. They were to "be *subject* to rulers and authorities, to be *obedient,*" and "to be *ready* to do whatever is *good.*" And toward *all* unbelievers they were "to be *peaceable* and *considerate,* and to show true humility" (3:1,2).

Paul anticipated that some of the Cretan believers might ask Titus *why* he insisted on this kind of life style among unbelievers. Consequently, he proceeded to spell out a theological basis for such behavior. First, Paul reasoned on the basis of a Christian's unsaved condition *in the past*—before he was converted to Christ. Second, he argued for a godly life style in various relationships with non-Christians because of God's work in our lives *in the present.* Notice Paul's argument as it is developed point by point.

A. Our Unsaved Condition in the Past

1. *We were foolish*

"At one time," Paul wrote, "we too were foolish." He was reminding Titus and those to whom he was ministering that all of us were without spiritual understanding when we were yet unconverted. Our "foolish hearts were darkened" (Rom. 1:21). We were dead in our "transgressions and sins" (Eph. 2:1). The Holy Spirit had not yet enlightened our hearts and minds. And as Paul reminded the Corinthians, "The man without the Spirit does not accept the things that come from the Spirit of God, for they are foolishness to him, and he cannot understand them, because they are spiritually discerned" (1 Cor. 2:14). Because we too were once in this condition, reasoned Paul, we should, of all people, understand non-Christians and be sensitive to them.

2. *We were disobedient*

Though this is the same word Paul used earlier in this Epistle to describe the incredible behavior of false teachers in Crete (Titus 1:16), he no doubt had a more comprehensive meaning in mind here. There are different levels of "disobedience," but in the final analysis whatever violates God's will is still disobedience. Except for the Lord Jesus Christ, there is no person living today—or who has ever lived, or who will ever live—who has not been guilty of disobeying God. This was Paul's conclusion in his letter to the Romans. "*All* have sinned and *fall short* of the glory of God" (Rom. 3:23). We have all missed the mark. "There is no one righteous, not even one" (Rom. 3:10). We have all disobeyed God at some point in our lives, bringing separation between ourselves and God. Again, knowing this should make us sensitive in the way we respond to non-Christians.

3. *We were deceived*

Here Paul was expanding on every person's lost condition. Being deceived suggests being led astray by a false guide or teacher. Not only is there in every human being an inherent tendency to do wrong because of our old sin nature inherited from Adam, but we are vulnerable to false influences from others. Our tendency is to imbibe the teachings and philosophy of this world rather than God's truth.

This is a tragic condition. Every human being born into this world finds himself in this state. There are no exceptions. A Christian who truly understands what he has been delivered from can only praise God that he has been set free from this kind of predicament. It is only because of his "new nature," which he has received from God, that he can begin to conform his life to Jesus Christ in a way that honors the Lord. Again, this in no way allows room for pride and arrogance in our relationship with non-Christians.

4. *We were enslaved*

Paul often used the metaphor of slavery to illustrate our condition both before and after we became Christians. Before knowing Christ, we were "enslaved by all kinds of passions and pleasures" (Titus 3:3); after knowing Christ, we were able to "*serve* one another in love" (Gal. 5:13). Before conversion, we were "slaves to sin" (Rom. 6:7); after conversion, we can "serve in the new way of the Spirit" (Rom. 7:6).

Again, there are degrees of "bondage" in which nonbelievers find themselves. Once a person gives himself over to sinful "passions and pleasures," the tentacles of sin tightened. This no doubt describes the Cretans who were noted for their *lying,* their *evil* deeds, and their *gluttony* (Titus 1:12). And if they had continued on their present course, they would have become like those described in Romans 1, whose condition became so perverse that God gave them over to "sexual impurity," "shameful lusts," and a "depraved mind" (Rom. 1:24,26,28).

But even Paul, a man who knew the law of God and desperately tried to obey it, found himself in bondage. Thus he wrote, "So then, I myself in my mind am a *slave* to God's law, but in my sinful nature a *slave* to the law of sin" (Rom. 7:25). No matter what our religious background, we can be set "free from the law of sin and death" only by God's Spirit as we put our faith in Jesus Christ (Rom. 8:2). This is why Paul includes "himself" in this letter to Titus. "At one time," he wrote, "*we too* were foolish, disobedient, deceived and enslaved by all kinds of passions and pleasures" (Titus 3:3). No matter what our religious and nonreligious heritage, we should be able to understand the non-Christian and have compassion on him. We should do all we can to love him and to relate to him in a way that will reveal our new life in Christ. In essence, if not in every way, we were once in his condition. And God desires to use us to set him "free" from his bondage.

5. *We lived in malice*

A person characterized by "malice" has a deep-seated desire to make others suffer. In fact, this kind of person experiences real satisfaction either in causing suffering or in observing it. And even Paul had to acknowledge that in his religious zeal as an unsaved Jew and as a dedicated Pharisee, he gained real satisfaction from persecuting the followers of Jesus Christ. But when he was converted to Jesus Christ, he was terribly ashamed of his behavior. This is the basic reason why Paul felt such a burden and responsibility to communicate the gospel to others. He knew it was only God's grace that had saved him. "I became a servant of this gospel by the gift of God's grace given me through the working of his power," he wrote to the Ephesians. "Although I am less than the least of all God's people, this grace was given me: to preach to the Gentiles the unsearchable riches of Christ" (Eph. 3:7-8).

Paul asks all Christians to have this same perspective, to feel a burden for non-Christians who are trapped in the same sins that at one time trapped them. Furthermore, this attitude will aid all of us in relating to non-Christians with understanding and kindness and, when necessary, with an attitude of submission and obedience.

6. *We lived in envy*

Envy represents a specific kind of malice and ill will. Envious people feel unhappiness, anger, and jealousy toward others because of their advantages.

Non-Christians easily fall into this sin, since they have no new nature. And though the old nature is capable of doing some "good" things if it is influenced by Christian values, it is much more easily influenced by negative examples. It can quickly reflect envy, a desire for what others have. And what makes it destructive is our desire to hurt others because they have what we want.

The world is filled with this kind of person, even in places of leadership. How should a Christian respond? Though the Bible nowhere tells us to condone these attitudes and actions, it does instruct us to be understanding. We, too, were once controlled by the same old nature.

7. *We lived in hatred*

"Being hated and hating one another" is the natural result of "malice and envy." In fact, it is a result of all the previous characteristics enumerated by Paul. According to the apostle John, *hatred* is the most basic characteristic for evaluating whether or not a person is a Christian:

> Anyone who claims to be in the light but hates his brother is still in the darkness. Whoever loves his brother lives in the

> light, and there is nothing in him to make him stumble. But whoever hates his brother is in the darkness and walks around in the darkness; he does not know where he is going, because the darkness has blinded him" (1 John 2:9-11).

B. God's Work in Our Lives in the Present

After reviewing those things that characterized all of us as non-Christians, at least to one degree or another, Paul turned to the theological basis for having proper attitudes and actions toward unbelievers. In many respects what he wrote is what he had just written in a previous section of the letter—what God's *grace* teaches us about the Christian life style (Titus 2:11-14). In this paragraph before us (3:4-7), however, Paul elaborates on what God's grace actually did for us.

2. *We were saved by grace*

Paul's main thrust in verses 4-7 stands out boldly against the backdrop formed by the non-Christian life style, which he has just described in verse 3. That is, we certainly were not saved by works: "not because of righteous things we had done." It was purely because of God's "mercy," which had as its source his "kindness" and "love." It was "while we were still sinners" that "Christ died for us" (Rom. 5:8).

The statement "he washed us through the washing of rebirth" has caused some discussion among Bible interpreters. Some feel Paul was referring here to water baptism as a means of God's grace in saving us. If this were true and a necessary part of salvation, we are hard put to explain the fact that this kind of baptism is administered by man, making his actions a necessary part of the process of salvation. This hardly correlates with the concept of "salvation by grace . . . through faith" that Paul is emphasizing in this passage and which also permeates the New Testament, including the fact that even Old Testament saints were made righteous by faith apart from works (Rom. 4:13,14).

Furthermore, if it were true that water baptism is a part of the process of salvation, we would also be hard put to explain the nebulous description of baptism in the New Testament—a nebulousness that is obvious because of the variety of opinions regarding the nature and form of baptism among noted Bible scholars.

It is far more logical from the whole of Scripture to interpret Paul's statement here as the eternal "cleansing" that takes place when we are regenerated by God's Spirit as a response to the *truth* He brought to light when He was sent into this world by Jesus Christ (John 14:17; 15:26; 16:2). The Holy Spirit in a very unique way revealed to us the "Word of God." And it is the Word of God that has become the divine means whereby we can be "born again" and "cleansed" from our sin. It is through the Word of God that we learn of Christ's redemptive work at the cross. As Peter stated, "For you have been *born again,* not of perishable seed, but of imperishable, through the living and enduring *word of God*" (1 Peter 1:23; see also 1 Cor. 6:11).

2. *We are being renewed by the Holy Spirit*

When we respond to God's grace by faith, we were not only justified by His grace and regenerated by the Holy Spirit, but there began a process by which we are continually being renewed by the Spirit. When the Spirit was "poured out on us generously through Jesus Christ our Savior" (Titus 3:6—a direct reference to His coming at Pentecost; see Acts 2:33), he then began the divine process of communicating to us through selected individuals (particularly the apostles) all that we need to know to become conformed to the image of Jesus Christ. As Paul reminded Timothy, "All Scripture is God-breathed and is useful for teaching, rebuking, correcting and training in righteousness, so that the man of God may be thoroughly equipped for every good work" (2 Tim. 3:16,17). Furthermore, Paul stated to the Romans: "Do not conform any longer to the pattern of this world, but be transformed *by the renewing* of your mind. Then you will be able to test and approve what God's will is—his good, pleasing and perfect will" (Rom. 12:2).

In summary, then, in Titus 3:3-7 Paul told Titus that we who are Christians should be sensitive to non-Christians and respond to them properly because we were once like them. But God saved us from our lost condition, not because of our works, but because of His mercy and grace. Therefore, we have no right to respond to their weaknesses by being rebellious and disobedient. Rather, we should "be ready to do whatever is good, to slander no one, to be peaceable and considerate, and to show true humility toward all men" (Titus 3:2).

A TWENTIETH-CENTURY APPLICATION AND LIFE RESPONSE

1. *A Primary application*

In the previous lesson application we dealt with our behavior toward all non-Christians, but particularly toward twentieth-century authority figures. The most obvious application from the passage in this lesson is an extension of our last lesson. It can be focused with one basic question: "How does a knowledge of God's grace in saving us when we were once like the non-Christians we work for and work with affect our attitudes and actions toward them?" If it does not cause us to respond more graciously and sensitively toward them, there is one logical conclusion—probably we do not have a proper appreciation of God's saving grace in our own lives.

Let's think about that for a moment. The most logical response of many Christians who have been reared in an environment affected by Christian truth is that they cannot identify with the pagan life style described by Paul in Titus 3:3. They do not view themselves as ever having been "foolish, disobedient, deceived and enslaved by all kinds of passions and pleasures." They have never "lived in malice, and envy, being hated and hating one another."

For many this may be true—at least when compared with the Cretan life style. But we can be absolutely sure of this, that it was only God's grace that kept us from "stepping over the edge" and experiencing the depths of sin into which many have fallen. It was only by God's grace we were reared in a Christian home, having Christian parents who modeled Christlike behavior that attracted us to Christ. And furthermore, remember that we are all sinners, no matter what our heritage. We have all fallen short of God's standard in some area of our life. And it took Christ's death on the cross and His shed blood to save us too. He paid the same price for our failures as He did for those who are wallowing in the mire of sin. This in itself should cause us to respond with compassion to those who have not been as fortunate as we.

2. *A Secondary application*

There is another area in which the truth of this passage crosses our lives as twentieth-century Christians. How does your life style as a Christian compare with the non-Christian life style described by Paul? Throughout the New Testament, believers are constantly exhorted to "put off" the "old self" and to "put on the new self, created to be like God in true righteousness and holiness" (Eph. 4:22,24). Consider the following passages and use them as a *personal life response*. Underscore any areas in your life where you need to conform more to Christ's image—particularly in relationship to non-Christians.

Ephesians 4:25-32

Therefore, each of you must put off falsehood and speak truthfully to his neighbor, for we are all members of one body. In your anger do not sin: Do not let the sun go down while you are still angry, and do not give the devil a foothold. He who has been stealing must steal no longer, but must work, doing something useful with his own hands, that he may have something to share with those in need.

Do not let any unwholesome talk come out of your mouths, but only what is helpful for building others up according to their needs, that it may benefit those who listen. And do not grieve the Holy Spirit of God, with whom you were sealed for the day of redemption. Get rid of all bitterness, rage and anger, brawling and slander, along with every form of malice. Be kind and compassionate to one another, forgiving each other, just as in Christ God forgave you.

Colossians 3:5-9

Put to death, therefore, whatever belongs to your earthly nature: sexual immorality, impurity, lust, evil desires and greed, which is idolatry. Because of these, the wrath of

God is coming. You used to walk in these ways, in the life you once lived. But now you must rid yourselves of all such things as these: anger, rage, malice, slander, filthy language. Do not lie to each other, since you have taken off your old self with its practices.

1 Peter 2:1-3

Therefore, rid yourselves of all malice and all deceit, hypocrisy, jealousy, and slander of every kind. Like newborn babies, crave pure spiritual milk, so that by it you may grow up in your salvation, now that you have tasted that the Lord is good.

Philippians 2:14,15

Do everything without complaining or arguing, so that you may become blameless and pure, children of God without fault in a crooked and depraved generation, in which you shine like stars in the universe.

Chapter XIII

Some Final Exhortations

SOMETHING TO THINK ABOUT

What actions do you feel are most prevalent in the average church when facing a problem with a "divisive" person?

- ☐ Ignore the person
- ☐ Confront the person in love
- ☐ Talk behind the person's back
- ☐ Develop resentment towards the person
- ☐ Deal with symptoms rather than with root problems
- ☐ Other __________

A LOOK AT PAUL'S LETTER

Stress What Is Profitable

3:8 This is a trustworthy saying. ——— 1
And I want you to stress these things,
so that those
who have trusted in God
may be careful
to devote themselves
to doing what is good.
These things are excellent
and
profitable
for everyone. } ——— 2

Avoid What Is Unprofitable

3:9 But avoid foolish controversies ——— 1
and
genealogies ——— 2
and
arguments ——— 3
and
quarrels about the law —4
because these are unprofitable
and
useless.

Deal With Divisive People

3:10 Warn a divisive person once, ——— 1
and
then warn him a second time. ——— 2
After that, have nothing to do with him. ——— 3
3:11 You may be sure that such a man is warped
and
sinful;
he is self-condemned.

WHAT DID PAUL SAY?

A. Stress What Is Profitable

1. God's Word is trustworthy
2. God's Word is profitable

B. Avoid What Is Unprofitable

1. Foolish controversies
2. Genealogies
3. Arguments
4. Quarrels

C. Deal With Divisive People

1. Warn once
2. Warn twice
3. Break fellowship

WHAT DID PAUL MEAN?

As Paul began to conclude this letter to Titus, his final exhortations were actually a recapitulation—some succinct statements summarizing what he had been emphasizing to this point. In the verses before us Paul exhorted Titus to stress what was *profitable* (3:8), to avoid what was *unprofitable* (3:9), and to deal with *divisive* people in a straightforward, but proper manner (3:10,11). In essence, these three statements represent why Paul left Titus in Crete in the first place (1:5) and why he wrote this letter.

A. Stress What Is Profitable

In verses 4-7 Paul had just stated the heart of the Christian message—that all Christians have the hope of eternal life, not because of our works of righteousness, but because of God's love, His mercy, and His grace. Furthermore, not only were we regenerated by the Holy Spirit when we believed in Christ, but we can be renewed and conformed to Christ's image right now. "This," wrote Paul, bridging the gap between these verses and those before us in this lesson, "is a *trustworthy saying*" (3:8). And, as we have already noted in a previous lesson, the reason this statement is "trustworthy" is that it is God's revealed truth.

1. *God's Word is trustworthy*

The phrase "trustworthy saying" or "trustworthy message" is not a new concept with Paul, even in this letter. Earlier Paul had instructed Titus to make sure that those who were to serve as elders in Crete were men who held "firmly to the *trustworthy message*." Without doubt, the apostle was referring to God's revealed Word—a message that could be trusted and relied on because of its divine source.

Though the "trustworthy message" probably refers to all of God's revealed truth, at this juncture in the letter Paul was undoubtedly referring to the "trustworthy saying" embodied in his previous theological statement regarding Christ's love and mercy in saving undeserving sinners (3:4-7). And this conclusion can be supported by other similar statements by

Paul, especially in his letters to Timothy. And in each case the theological statement *follows* rather than *precedes* the phrase "this is a trustworthy saying." Note also that in each case, the theological statement is in essence the same statement as in his letter to Titus:

> "Here is a *trustworthy saying* that deserves full acceptance: Christ Jesus came into the world to save sinners—of whom I am the worst. But for that very reason I was shown mercy so that in me, the worst of sinners, Christ Jesus might display his unlimited patience as an example for those who would believe on him and receive eternal life" (1 Tim. 1:15-16).
>
> "This is a *trustworthy saying* that deserves full acceptance (and for this we labor and strive), that we have put our hope in the living God, who is the Savior of all men, and especially of those who believe" (1 Tim. 4:9,10).
>
> "Here is a *trustworthy saying:* If we died with him, we will also live with him; if we endure, we will also reign with him. If we disown him, he will also disown us, if we are faithless, he will remain faithful, for he cannot disown himself" (2 Tim. 2:11-13).

In each instance in the letters to Timothy as well as in the letter to Titus, the "trustworthy saying" involved the message of redemption and salvation. Though stating it differently in each instance, Paul was reiterating basically the same "trustworthy saying."

2. *God's Word is profitable*

Paul next moved for a *particular* truth—indeed the most important truth in the whole of Scripture—to the *total* message he had been communicating to Titus. "And I want you to stress *these things*" (3:8). Here Paul was referring to everything he had written in this letter—the truth regarding his own calling as an apostle, the qualifications for elders (which Paul also classified as a "trustworthy saying" in 1 Timothy 3:1), how to handle false teachers, godly characteristics for a Christian life style for *all* Christians, and, as just stated, the theological basis for this Christian life style.

In 3:8 Paul also summarized the purpose for stressing

"these things"—"so that those who have trusted in God may be careful to devote themselves *to doing what is good.*" This was indeed Paul's greatest concern throughout this Epistle. He was called not only to preach the message of "eternal life" and how to receive it but also to communicate the whole counsel of God regarding a Christian life style. *All* of God's Word is important. Thus Paul wrote, "These *things* [*all* I have stated] are excellent and *profitable*" (3:8b).

When Paul wrote his second letter to Timothy, he left no questions about how he viewed God's written revelation and its purpose. "*All Scripture,*" he wrote, "is God-breathed and is *useful* [that is, profitable] for teaching, rebuking, correcting and training in righteousness, so that the man of God may be thoroughly equipped *for every good work*" (2 Tim. 3:16). This was also Paul's great concern in his letter to Titus. Consequently, he exhorted Titus to "stress these things." Why? Because "*these things* are excellent and *profitable.*"

B. Avoid What Is Unprofitable

To make sure Titus clearly understood his task, Paul spelled out *those things* he was to avoid and *not* to stress—"foolish controversies and genealogies and arguments and quarrels about the law."

There were many false teachers in the New Testament world who were emphasizing these very things (see also 1 Tim. 1:4; 6:3-5; 2 Tim. 2:14; 23-26). Paul had already dealt with these issues earlier in his letter when he told Titus how to deal with false teachers. He called them "rebellious people, *mere talkers* and *deceivers,* especially of the *circumcision group*" (1:10). And included in the "things" they were teaching that they "ought not to teach" were "Jewish myths" (1:11,14). There were individuals in Crete who were teaching false doctrine. Many of them were evidently Gentiles who had mixed certain aspects of Judaism with elements from their pagan religions and had produced a syncretistic message that was very appealing but very dangerous. And in some subtle way (which is also true in the twentieth century) it caused people to pay money in order to get involved (1:11).

It is not possible to reconstruct specifically the content of their message, one reason being that there were probably as many variations in their doctrines as there were false teachers. This can also be said about false teachers and their message in the twentieth century.

Titus was to avoid these false doctrines, "foolish controversies and genealogies" because false doctrine always leads to "arguments and quarrels," whereas God's truth spoken in love leads to doctrinal stability, "unity in the faith" and a demonstration of Christian love (Eph. 4:11-16). Putting it another way, God's Word is *profitable* (3:8b); false doctrine is always *unprofitable* (3:9b).

C. Deal With Divisive People

How was Titus to handle people who were involved in propagating false doctrine? Earlier he had generalized, stating that "they must be silenced" (1:11). Titus was to "rebuke them sharply" (1:13). But as Paul began to culminate his letter, he felt it was necessary to be more specific, one reason being that not all of those dabbling in false doctrine were in the same class as those Paul described in the earlier part of the letter. Those he wrote about in chapter 1 were prominent leaders who were already "ruining whole households." They already had been "weighed in the balance and found wanting." It was clear that they were not true believers in that they were corrupt in "both their minds and consciences" (1:15). In dealing with them, there was only one recourse for Titus—radical surgery. They must be stopped. If they were not, many more immature Christians would be led astray.

However, there were no doubt so-called believers in Crete who had been influenced by these "detestable and disobedient" individuals (1:16), but who had not yet been evaluated by a proper biblical procedure. It was necessary to test the degree of their commitment to false doctrine and the depth of their involvement. Thus Paul concludes his letter by spelling out a clear-cut process.

First, how do you recognize such a person? Paul answered this question clearly: He is "divisive" (3:10). As Paul reminded Timothy, who was in Ephesus at the time, *myths* and *endless genealogies* "promote controversies" (1 Tim. 1:4).

There is another way, however, to recognize false teachers. What they teach not only creates divisiveness, but it eventually leads to ungodliness. This is why Paul warned Timothy to "avoid godless chatter, because those who indulge in it will become more and more ungodly" (2 Tim. 2:16). The true test of a person's ministry is that it produces not only converts but also a Christlike life style. The false teachers in Crete were doing the opposite, primarily because they themselves were denying God by their actions, even though they claimed to know Him (1:16).

But Paul deals with a second question. How do you handle such a person? Again, Paul's answer is clear. He must be warned, not only once but at least twice (3:10). And then if he does not respond, we must break fellowship with him. To quote Paul, we are "to have nothing to do with him." We are not to allow ourselves to get involved in his unprofitable activities.

Paul spelled this out even more clearly in his letter to Timothy:

> Flee the evil desires of youth, and pursue righteousness, faith, love and peace, along with those who call on the Lord out of a *pure* heart. Don't have anything to do with foolish and stupid arguments, because you know they produce quarrels. And the Lord's servant must not quarrel; instead, he must be kind to everyone, able to teach, not resentful. Those who oppose him he must gently instruct, in the hope that God will give them a change of heart leading them to a knowledge of the truth, and that they will come to their senses and escape from the trap of the devil, who has taken them captive to do his will" (2 Tim. 2:22-26).

But there will be those who will not respond to gentle warnings but will continue to be divisive. And if they do, *then* we "may be sure that such a man is warped and sinful:

he is self-condemned'' (Titus 3:11). As Paul stated earlier, he has demonstrated with his life style that he is ''unfit for doing anything good'' (1:16). He has brought judgment on himself and ''must be silenced.'' If he is not, his teaching ''will spread like gangrene'' (2 Tim. 2:17), and many immature Christians (and non-Christians) will be led astray. In such cases, Paul himself did not hesitate to deal with the problem directly and firmly.

A TWENTIETH-CENTURY APPLICATION

The summary exhortations given by Paul to Titus in this passage of Scripture certainly have direct relevance to every believer's life today. Consider the following questions:

1. To what extent do you *stress those things that are profitable,* both in your own life and for others?

   Perhaps there is an even more basic question that every Christian needs to ask and answer. Twice in Paul's first letter to Timothy, he stated, ''Here is a trustworthy saying *that deserves full acceptance*'' (1 Tim. 1:15; 4:9). To what extent do you actually accept God's Word in the Bible as authoritative in your life? Note, I did not say to what extent do you believe it *is* God's Word, but rather, to what extent have you *received* it and committed your life to it?

   There is the same basic difference between those who *believe* that Christ is the Son of God and those who have *accepted* Him personally as Savior and Lord. This is the difference between being a true Christian and a Christian in ''name only.'' But there are also true Christians who believe the Bible is God's Word, but they have not brought their lives under its complete authority. They acknowledge its trustworthiness, but they have not allowed themselves to respond with ''full acceptance.'' What about you?

   This leads to another important observation. Christians who accept the Bible in theory but not in practice do not and cannot communicate it with a sense of true conviction and authority to others. Their words have a hollow ring. Both Paul and Titus could "stress these things" with others only because they had "stressed them" in their own lives. As James stated, "Show me your faith without deeds, and I will show you my faith by what I do" (James 2:18b).

Two more related questions, particularly for those directly involved in the ministry: To what extent do you emphasize God's grace in salvation but neglect what the Bible teaches regarding holiness? On the other hand, to what extent do you emphasize "works" and neglect what the Bible teaches about God's grace? Both emphases are essential. If they are not properly balanced in our ministry, we are not teaching "the whole counsel of God." To be sure, we are only saved by grace through faith. Salvation is a gift of God (Eph. 2:8,9). But it is also true that "we are God's workmanship, created in Christ Jesus *to do good works,* which God prepared in advance for us to do" (Eph. 2:10).

2. To what extent do you avoid what is "unprofitable?"

Some Christians dwell on peripheral issues and secondary matters in the Christian faith. They get emotional satisfaction from creating controversy. Rather than making "every effort to keep the unity of the spirit through the bond of peace" (Eph. 4:3), they do what they can to create divisions and disunity. Paul classifies this kind of behavior among Christians as "worldly" (1 Cor. 3:1-3). What about your life? How do *you* measure up?

NOTE: Some Christians engage in this kind of behavior because they are uninformed and ignorant regarding what the Bible really teaches. Some do it, however, because of emotional and spiritual problems. They want to be the center of attention. And then there are some who—like the Cretan false teachers, do it "for the sake of dishonest gain" (Titus 1:11). Their motives are totally materialistic and selfish. These three levels of behavior illustrate why Paul suggested a definite procedure for dealing with people who are divisive. Those who are ignorant of God's truth but are sincere will respond to the truth when confronted with it.

3. To what extent do you follow the scriptural procedure and process for dealing with divisive people?

The Bible directs this question more specifically to spiritual leaders in the church. Paul exhorted the Ephesian elders to "guard" themselves and "all the flock" over whom the Holy Spirit had made them overseers. They were to be "shepherds of the church of God" (Acts 20:28).

In many churches spiritual leaders tend to ignore problems. They hesitate to face reality with people who are causing divisions. And by ignoring such problems, they are not only disobeying God but also failing to protect other believers who may be led astray. They are opening the door to all kinds of problems.

On the other hand, elders and pastors are not the only ones responsible to deal with these problems. It is clear from Scripture that *all* Christians are responsible to teach and counsel one another. This is why Paul stated to the Colossians: "Let the word of Christ dwell in you richly as you teach and counsel one another with all wisdom" (Col. 3:16).

NOTE: A Christian must not try to take "a speck of sawdust" out of his brother's eye when he has a "plank" in his own eye. Jesus calls one who tries to do that a hypocrite (Matt. 7:3-5). However, it must also be pointed out that spiritual problems in our own lives do not give us a persistent "escape route" for avoiding our responsibility for other Christians. If we are to walk in God's will, we must indeed live according to God's will. And as we do, a part of our responsibility as members of the body of Christ is to care for others and help them also walk in the will of God.

A PERSONAL LIFE RESPONSE

Reflect again on the twentieth-century application and

isolate the areas in your life where you need some improvement. Write out one goal and a step you can take to reach that goal so that you will be able to be more obedient to God's Word immediately.

Chapter XIV

Paul's Closing Remarks

SOMETHING TO THINK ABOUT

What phrase would you use to describe Titus's official position in the church in Crete:

- ☐ An apostle
- ☐ The pastor
- ☐ An evangelist
- ☐ An elder
- ☐ A teacher
- ☐ An apostolic representative
- ☐ Other ________

A LOOK AT PAUL'S LETTER

Paul's Future Plans for Titus

3:12 As soon as I send Artemas
or
Tychicus to you,
do your best to come to me at Nicolopis,
because I have decided to winter there.

A Challenge to Show Christian Hospitality

3:13 Do everything you can to help Zenas the lawyer
and
Apollos
on their way
and
see that they have everything they need.

3:14 Our people must learn to devote themselves
to doing what is good,
in order that they may provide for daily necessities
and
not live unproductive lives.

Paul's Final Greetings

3:15 Everyone with me sends greetings.
Greet those who love us in the faith.
Grace be with you all.

WHAT DID PAUL SAY?

A. Paul's Future Plans for Titus

B. A Challenge to Show Christian Hospitality

C. Paul's Final Greetings

WHAT DID PAUL MEAN?

Paul ended his letter to Titus in a rather typical fashion. He gave some final instructions both to Titus personally and to the Cretans generally. He then concluded with some very personal greetings.

On first reading, it may appear that there is little we can learn from Paul's closing remarks. However, a closer look at these verses in relationship to the larger context of this letter and others that Paul wrote bring to the surface several very important principles. The first has to do with Paul's *discipling procedures,* the second with *church government,* and the third with the concept of *Christian hospitality.*

A. Paul's Future Plans for Titus

Following his basic work of evangelism on the island of Crete, Paul had left Titus there to "straighten out what was left unfinished," that is, to care for matters that still needed attention in order to help the Cretan Christians become a mature and thriving body of believers. His task was twofold: first, Titus was to "appoint elders in every town" (Titus 1:5). These were to be godly men who could pastor the new believers and counteract the negative influence of false teachers who were already at work "ruining whole households" (1:11). Second, he was to "teach what is in accord with sound doctrine" (2:1—in short, to teach the new believers *how to live* as Christians in view of God's redeeming love, mercy, and grace.

It appears that Titus was already well along in carrying out these responsibilities when he received Paul's letter. This Epistle simply served as a more detailed reminder of what Paul and Titus had no doubt talked about before Paul departed from Crete. Furthermore, it served as an authoritative document to lend support and apostolic significance to Titus's work.

Titus's ministry in Crete, however, was temporary. Paul had other plans for him. Consequently, he wrote, "As soon as I send Artemas or Tychicus to you, do your best to come to me at Nicopolis, because I have decided to winter there" (Titus 3:12).

Note several important things about this verse. First, Titus had not brought the work he was assigned to do far enough along to leave it unattended. Consequently, Paul was going to send a replacement. It would be either Artemas or Tychicus.

We know nothing of Artemas other than this mention of his name in this letter. We can conclude, however, that he must have been a very mature Christian to be considered as a replacement for Titus, especially in view of the problems Titus had been facing in Crete. Furthermore, to be considered along with Tychicus for this work also adds support to this conclusion. Tychicus we *do* know. He was from the "province of Asia" and was one of several choice men who traveled with Paul as a missionary companion (Acts 20:2-6). He was intimately acquainted with Paul's affairs and on several occasions traveled to various churches for the express purpose of communicating to them how Pual was doing personally and also of reporting on his missionary activities. For example, Paul wrote in the final paragraph in his letter to the Ephesians: "Tychicus, the dear brother and faithful servant in the Lord, will tell you everything, so that you also may know *how I am* and *what I am doing*. I am sending him to you for this very purpose, that you may know how we are, and that he may encourage you" (Eph. 6:21-22; see also Col. 4:7-9 and 2 Tim. 4:12).

It appears that Paul's goal was to send either Tychicus or Artemas to Crete, probably to report on Paul's own welfare and ministry, but primarily to continue Titus's organizing and teaching ministry. Titus was to leave Crete and join Paul in Nicopolis, probably the city of that name in Epirus. Paul's plan was to spend the winter there.

We are not sure what Paul had in mind for Titus except that he wanted his faithful Christian companion to be with him. While he was in Rome, he had a similar request of Timothy: "Do your best to get here before *winter*" (2 Tim. 4:21).

In both situations we know that Paul was no longer a young

man. He knew his time on earth might be short. It would be logical to conclude that he wanted to spend time during the winter months continuing the training of both Titus and Timothy, communicating everything he had learned, both by direct revelation from God and experientially in the ministry. We know this was one of Paul's primary concerns, which is expressed well in his second letter to Timothy: "And the things you have heard me say in the presence of many witnesses entrust to reliable men who will also be qualified to teach others" (2 Tim. 2:2)

Both Titus and Timothy reflect Paul's *discipling ministry and strategy*. While he was carrying out the Great Commission and planting churches all over the New Testament world, he was building the lives of others for the work of service—but especially these two young men. Paul's desire was that they continue his work after he was gone. In essence this reflects the example of Christ, who built His life into twelve men to carry on His work after His ministry on earth was ended. But it is clear that two men were especially called and prepared by Christ—Peter and John. Other than Paul himself, they are clearly the most prominent apostles in the book of Acts. Like Christ, then, Paul first had a ministry at large, he also had a more in-depth ministry with a larger group of men, and finally he had a very concentrated ministry to Timothy and Titus. With these men he no doubt spent quality time, perhaps during the winter months when his ministry at large was somewhat curtailed.

There is a second significant implication that emerges from Paul's future plans for Titus. It relates to *church government*. Paul's goal was to bring a given church to the place where it could function with its own elders or pastors without assistance from "a Timothy" or "a Titus." Though the Christians at Crete were not yet ready for this phase in their growth and maturity, Titus had laid the groundwork. Evidently he was well on his way in appointing qualified "elders in every town" and had been teaching "what is in accord with sound doctrine." Artemas or Tychicus would continue that work when Titus left to join Paul in Nicopolis. The next step, however, would be for the Cretan elders to carry on the work by themselves.

This does not mean that there would not be men serving full time in the ministry at Crete. The natural process would be to recognize men who were "worthy of double honor"—men who spent most of their time "preaching and teaching" (2 Tim. 5:17). According to the Scriptures, they should be remunerated for their efforts. They were comparable to what we call in our culture "full-time pastors."

One other important aspect regarding church government that is reflected in Paul's letter to Titus as well as in other places in the New Testament is the concept of multiple leadership. It seems that it was Paul's goal for every New Testament church to have more than one elder or pastor managing a local body of believers. Interestingly, we never find the singular word *elder* used in describing leadership in the church. Rather, the New Testament refers to "the elders" of the church.

It must be recognized, however, that church structures were quite different in the New Testament world, one reason being that it was difficult if not impossible to own property and build buildings as we do today. Consequently, in some situations there were a number of "house churches" that made up a given body of believers or "church" in a particular geographical location. In a given city or town there might be a number of small groups that were designated as "the church" in such a city. Beyond this, it is difficult to reconstruct structural forms. For example, in Crete Titus was to "appoint elders in every town." Does this mean there were a number of small churches in each town with an elder over each one? Or was there an elder in every town, serving more than one house church?

We do not know the specific answers to these questions. One thing is clear however. Multiple leadership of any group of Christians in a geographical area was the goal for New Testament church government. Titus's task, as well as Timothy's, was to help each church develop to this point, then move on to a new responsibility. In other words, neither

Timothy nor Titus served churches as permanent pastors. Both of these men did follow-up work for Paul. The goal was to create independent churches—churches with their own leadership, functioning bodies that ministered to themselves, a growing body of Christians who were maintaining a dynamic witness in the world. The "churches" in Crete are a unique example of this process. Titus was left there by Paul to help make it happen.

B. A Challenge to Show Christian Hospitality

Paul also had some final instructions for all the believers in Crete. Though spoken to Titus, the message was for the church: "Do everything you can to help Zenas the lawyer and Apollos on their way and see that they have everything they need" (Titus 3:13).

Zenas, the lawyer, like Artemas, is not a well-known New Testament Christian. This is the only time his name is mentioned, but, as with Artemas, we are given a clue as to his credibility and status as a Christian when he is mentioned along with Apollos.

Apollos was a native of Alexandria and before he fully understood the gospel of God's grace he was teaching about Jesus Christ's life on this earth. Even at this point in his life Luke describes him as "a learned man, with a thorough knowledge of the Scriptures" (Acts 18:24).

But Apollos knew "only the baptism of John." One day a husband-and-wife team, Aquila and Priscilla, heard Apollos teaching. Recognizing his great skill but limited knowledge, they invited him to their home where they "explained to him the way of God more adequately" (Acts 18:26). Consequently, Apollos became a great Christian apologist, in both evangelism and edification. As Luke records, "He vigorously refuted the Jews in public debate, proving from the Scriptures that Jesus was the Christ" (Acts 18:28).

Apollos, then, was a dynamic New Testament missionary, a man Paul trusted and supported. Evidently Zenas, who was probably a specialist in Roman law, was traveling with Apollos. Perhaps he had turned from his secular trade, either temporarily or permanently, in order to serve as a minister of the gospel. In one respect they had something in common with Paul and Titus respectively—that is, Apollos was a converted Jew and evidently Zenas was a converted Gentile.

Whatever the facts, these men were passing through Crete on a missionary tour, and Paul was concerned that their physical needs be met by the Christians in Crete. Consequently, he instructed Titus to see that this was done.

Paul then made another statement that seems to apply more generally to the concept of "Christian hospitality" and to helping missionaries in particular. "Our people," he wrote, "must learn to devote themselves to doing what is good, in order that they may provide for daily necessities and not live unproductive lives" (Titus 3:14).

"Doing what is good" and providing "for daily necessities" no doubt refers to Paul's previous injunction about helping Zenas and Apollos "on their way" and making sure "they have everything they need." Paul was desirous that the new believers have an opportunity to express their gratitude to God for their own salvation by helping the missionaries proclaim the gospel to others as well. Some of the Cretans had already been led astray financially in supporting "false teachers" (1:11). Paul was alerting them to the great opportunity to minister to two men who were indeed God's servants and worthy of their financial help

C. Paul's Final Greetings

Paul ended his letter to Titus with three succinct but very personal statements. First, *"Everyone with me sends you greetings"* (3:15a). We can only speculate regarding who was with Paul. Titus no doubt knew and could relate this information to the Cretan Christians. Otherwise, Paul would have probably mentioned specifically who these people were, just as he did in his other letters (Rom. 16:21-23; 1 Cor. 16:19; Phil. 4:22; 2 Tim. 4:21; Philem. 23).

Second, *"Greet those who love us in the faith"* (3:15b). Some translate this, "Greet those who love us as Christians." The reason for this translation is that the article is missing before "faith," and rather than referring to *the* Christian faith, Paul may have been referring to those who loved him and his co-workers "faithfully." In other words, Paul wanted to be remembered in a special way to those who were spiritually and emotionally involved with him in the ministry. Obviously, those reading or listening to this letter would know immediately if they qualified to be involved in this greeting.

Third, *"Grace be with you all"* (3:15c). Here Paul included all the Christians at Crete. This final greeting was a common one for Paul, and was nearly identical to his final words in 1 Timothy 6:20 and 2 Timothy 4:22. It was also a common greeting in the Gentile world, even among non-Christians. But every Cretan Christian knew Paul's final words represented more than just social protocol. "Grace" to Paul was a constant reminder of every Christian's position with Christ and of the fact that they were brothers and sisters in the family of God. It was *that* grace that gave them this position with God and with one another—not anything that they had done. Thus Paul wrote to the Ephesians:

> God raised us up with Christ and seated us with him in the heavenly realms in Christ Jesus, in order that in the coming ages he might show the *incomparable riches of his grace,* expressed in his kindness to us in Christ Jesus. For it is by *grace* you have been saved, through faith—and this not from yourselves, it is the gift of God—not by works, so that no one can boast. For we are God's workmanship, created in Christ Jesus to do good works, which God prepared in advance for us to do" (Eph. 2:6-10).

A TWENTIETH-CENTURY APPLICATION

The three principles that emerge from Paul's concluding remarks in many respects serve as a fitting conclusion to this entire letter. Paul's example in discipling, his emphasis on multiple leadership, and his view of Christian hospitality and missions all stand out as fundamental concepts in planting and building mature churches and in helping people of all ages to develop a Christian life style that is worthy of the calling they have received (Eph. 4:1). What does this say to us who live in the twentieth-century world?

1. Though the Bible does not give an absolute pattern for developing mature Christian leaders, it does illustrate a principle. *Without neglecting the body at large, we must build our lives into a few individuals who will multiply our efforts.* And it appears that even among these few, there will be one or two that will become a "Timothy" or a "Titus."

   This was certainly true in my own life. For a period of time a Christian leader by the name of Harold Garner took a keen interest in me while I was a student at Moody Bible Institute. He counseled me, prayed with me, and most of all motivated me to get involved in the ministry—to learn by experience. The greatest thing he did for me, however, was to believe in me when I was having trouble believing in myself. It changed my life.

   This leads to another very important observation. Paul's major ministry was not developing two men or even ten or twelve. His major effort was church planting and building up the saints generally. His special disciples learned the ministry while they were either with him or *not* with him, often going it alone. Their major growth came as a result of "experiencing" Christianity by facing the enemy on the front lines, by coming face to face with false teachers, by enduring criticisms and a hostile audience, by taking a group of Christians who were terribly immature and helping them to grow in Christ, and by developing men who could serve as spiritual leaders in the church.

   This is an important observation. There are too many people today who want to "be discipled" by observing and listening, not by participating in the process of evangelism and edification.

   Again, a Christian does not need an official position or platform in a church to carry out this process. Wherever there are people, saved or unsaved, there is a mission field. This is how Paul discovered Timothy. He was a dynamic member of Christ's body in Lystra. Consequently, "the brothers at Lystra *and* Iconium spoke well of him." And it was because of this reputation that "Paul wanted to take him along on the journey"—the second missionary tour where Timothy really began to learn the ministry firsthand (Acts 16:2-3). It was in this context that Timothy was able to demonstrate his willingness to "hang in there" when the going got tough. Timothy and Titus both passed the test and developed tremendous credibility with Paul. He would trust them with his own reputation.

On the other hand, John Mark had to learn his lesson the hard way. He quit in the middle of Paul's first missionary journey (Acts 13:13). Later, when Barnabas wanted to take him along on the second journey, Paul was skeptical. Luke has recorded Paul's thoughts and feelings clearly: "Barnabas wanted to take John, also called Mark, with them, but Paul did not think it wise to take him, because he had deserted them in Pamphylia and had not continued with them in the work" (Acts 15:37-38).

Mark evidently learned his lesson and proved himself even to Paul. There is no question where he stood with Jesus Christ. He was called by God to record the life of Jesus in the second Gospel. Fortunately, Barnabas still believed in him, and John Mark had a second chance. Later Paul demonstrated his own renewed confidence in him. Writing to Timothy, he said, "Get Mark and bring him with you, because he is helpful to me in my ministry" (2 Tim. 4:11). Paul did not feel comfortable with a "quitter," but he also recognized when a man had learned from his past mistakes. This in itself is a great lesson to all of us who are working with people.

2. Second, Paul's view of *multiple leadership in the church is basic to developing a mature body of believers*. Christians generally need many Christlike models—not just one. Furthermore, no single Christian leader can be a satisfactory model. We all have strengths and weakness-

es. Multiple elders and pastors together form a profile for people to emulate. Strengths and weaknesses are balanced through this important principle.

In addition, multiple leadership helps to counteract the tendency for some people to "worship" a dynamic leader. Having many Christlike men helps to diffuse this tendency. It is much easier to focus on Jesus Christ when He is reflected by "many" rather than by a single individual.

3. One very important aspect of "doing what is good" and demonstrating a Christian life style is *supporting others financially who desire to carry the good news of Christ to others*. Christians "*must* learn" this, wrote Paul. Otherwise, they will be living "unproductive lives" from the standpoint of eternal values.

   The Philippian Christians were an outstanding corporate example of what Paul was encouraging the Cretans to do. "For even when I was in Thessalonica," he wrote, "you sent me aid again and again when I was in need." And then Paul stated the most important factor in Christian stewardship, from the point of view both of the receiver and of the giver: "Not that I am looking for a gift, but I am looking for what may be credited to your account" (Phil. 4:16-17). The Philippians were investing not only in Paul, the man they loved, but also in the lives of many who would come to know Christ through his ministry. This is the fruit that would be "credited" to their account in the eternal bank of heaven.

A PERSONAL LIFE RESPONSE

The following questions are based on the above three principles and in turn become criteria by which any Christian can measure his Christian life style.

1. To what extent are you involved in the body of Christ, doing what you can to minister to others? Remember that you do not need an official role to minister to others. You already have an official role—a charter from Jesus Christ

Himself. What about the person sitting next to you?

2. Have you demonstrated sufficient commitment to Christ's body to warrant someone's taking a special interest in you as a personal disciple?
3. To what extent are you willing to learn the ministry through participation, facing the reality of hardships—even failure? How faithful are you when the going gets tough?
4. Do you have someone whom you are discipling? Have you ever thought about the fact that someone may be watching you and trying to learn how to live the Christian life?
5. What can you do to further the application of the principle of multiple leadership in the church?
6. To what extent are you a good steward of what God has given you, investing your time, your efforts, and your money in those who are anxious to carry the gospel to the ends of the earth?